WHAT JUST HAPPENED?

WHAT JUST HAPPENED?

Bitter Hollywood Tales from the Front Line

ART LINSON

BLOOMSBURY

Published by Bloomsbury, New York and London
Distributed to the trade by Holtzbrinck Publishers

First published in hardcover by Bloomsbury in 2002
Hardcover ISBN 1-58234-240-7

This paperback edition published in 2003
Paperback ISBN 1-58234-288-1

2 4 6 8 10 9 7 5 3 1

Typeset by Hewer Text Ltd
Printed in Great Britain by Clays Ltd, St Ives plc

For Fiona
for countless reasons

Contents

ONE

NEGATIVE PICKUP

'**B**og snorkeling, baby.'

'Huh?'

'I was grabbing the knee pads for decades.'

'Very colorful, Jerry, but not what I remember.'

'Every day in my office screaming, "Cesspool! Cesspool!" I thought you knew.'

'Knew what? You were on top.'

'It was a ruse.'

'Hey, a legend who quit before his time . . . takes big balls if you ask me.'

On the word *legend*, he blew me a kiss. His engine was starting to rev up now.

'Nonsense, I was eating the pound cake every day. That's right, every day, and thank you, I'm well out of it.'

'I . . . I never knew.'

But, of course, I did.

Jerry was sitting in a small booth in the rear of a Malibu coffee shop, one of those garden restaurants with bad lighting, across from the coast highway. It was breakfast time and the place was nearly empty. I had entered alone looking for a seat near the window where I could read the trades, but when our eyes met, the reunion became inevitable. Finding another table was not an option.

'So, how long has it been, Jerry? Two years, four years?'

'You think I count? For me, Hollywood and everyone in it died and I've never been happier, never.'

'Good.'

'Have a seat. Join me.'

I wasn't ready yet.

'Lookame . . . I'm so fuckin happy . . . c'mon, siddown.'

'Well . . . Jer, to me you'll always be the guy that told Ovitz that you were going to put him in the penalty box, and that's when he *was* Ovitz.'

'I did, didn't I?' Jerry grinned.

On that note, I could have graciously ended this exchange. No reason to start up this horror again, but I guess I couldn't resist. A look back at the past, revisiting one of the wasted. Who could resist?

Actually, at first I hadn't recognized Jerry. It had been only five years, but he seemed smaller, less square-jawed. Sudden loss of power, engines failing, and a public dumping could affect anyone's appearance. After all, wouldn't Katzenberg seem a whole lot smaller without a job? Standing awkwardly trying to figure my next move, I tried to hide *Variety* and *The Hollywood Reporter* inside my *New York Observer*. It was too late. I got the 'Oh, you still read that silly shit, do ya?' look as he patted the seat at the end of the banquette.

When I finally sat, he stood.

He pointed to his waist with his left hand and his chest with his right.

'Well?'

'What?'

'Look at me.'

'I am.'

'Pilates. I could lift this table and throw it through the kitchen and then touch my toes with my legs crossed.'

'Jerry, please sit down, I'm getting scared.'

'I'm so fit I could kick my son's ass.'

The last time I'd seen him, he was one of the few running Hollywood. You know that catch phrase *studio head*? Well, he was one of those. He had told me then that soon, very soon, he was going to get out. 'Get outta Hollywood and get *a life*.' He'd said that the losses were no longer salved by the victories. And Jerry had had some losses. Movies were bombing in bunches. They were his calls. Some of those movies I'd produced. He was starting to drink at lunch. He said that just reading the trades pushed him to the rim of rectal bleeding. There was no good news. If a story about him was negative, he shuddered. If an item aggrandized an acquaintance, his stomach tightened. Greed and envy grinding him up before noon. Near the end, his own staff struggled to make eye contact with him at the Monday-morning meetings.

When the bell tolls for studio heads, instead of jail time they get stock options. They get ceremoniously dumped and are soon forgotten. Being the effects of such a twisted system can beat the shit out of the very best – especially when the flow ain't quite going their way. Jerry was just another one of those guys on the chain.

He was big.

Was.

'Are you sayin' that you don't look back?'

'That's right,' he said.

I must say his bitterness was brilliantly concealed.

'Jerry, I don't mean in some sentimental way, but you know . . . out of curiosity.'

'Curiosity's not my thing.'

'C'mon, there's gotta be some tap dance on some grave tha—'

'I know where you're going. You think I want to get even with . . .'

'Last I recall, Jerry, retribution used to be your vitamins.'

'That chapter ended.'

'You were the one that said when I run somebody over, I want the cocksucker facing me so I can enjoy watching him experience the full impact.'

'Yoga. I've buried my anger.'

'Where?'

'I only see blue skies now.'

After ten minutes with Jerry, I couldn't avoid reflecting on my own Hollywood mortality. Let's face it, time was running out. In fact, the sand in the hourglass was hemorrhaging. For me, producing hit movies had become an increasingly farfetched affair. And in this town, where 'new' is best, I could feel that black hole of Hollywood purgatory waiting for me.

As I continued my catch-up with Jerry, my mind drifted. Strangely, I started to wonder if David Begelman had shot himself to avoid the nuisance of being alive while he was doing his time 'out of the biz.' Truly a show business conundrum. Begelman, who had neatly survived the embarrassment of embezzling money when he'd run Columbia Pictures, had had a much tougher time when his horsepower dried up. Apparently, after being deposed, the horror of not getting a CAA agent on the phone turned out to be life-threatening.

I looked back at Jerry.

'You could use a hit, by the way,' he said.

'Huh?'

Was that a vindictive remark? I couldn't tell. His mouth, filled with oatmeal, hid his expression. Was he telling me that I would soon join the pack of the dispossessed? I think so.

'What do you mean, I need a hit?'

'Trust me, you need a hit.'

His smile was slight but dangerous. He was surely vibing me with 'Get ready, you're next, *it's almost over*.' I admit I was vulnerable. It's not that I hadn't had my share of successes, but I'd just completed a

4

five-year run at Twentieth Century Fox, and to say that I'd left that incompetent brothel bloodied, scorched, defeated, and monumentally pissed off would be a grand understatement.

'Last I checked, everyone needs a hit,' I said.

'Especially you.'

'For someone so blissfully out of the game, how'd you know?'

'Your face gives it away.'

'I think not.'

I looked down at the menu.

'Actually it's a whole aura sort of thing,' he said. 'Once you know what to look for, it's as loud as acid-green paint.'

Perhaps I did feel a little rocky. I just didn't know that it showed at nine in the morning. I had to wonder, if success smells so sweet, what must the other thing smell like? I guess even a slim dose of desperation travels across the table.

'What would you like to order?' the waitress interrupted.

I started. 'Egg whites scrambled, tomatoes on the side, no potatoes, no bread, a side of well-done bacon, and black coffee.'

'Acid-green paint, clear as day.'

'What?'

'The protein thing. Holding on to the withering testosterone, are you?'

'Lookit . . . It's been five years and you're already pimping my diet. Jerry, don't let's turn this thing into some darker thing. It's too soon.'

Actually Jerry was raising some serious stuff. This wasn't going to be a lesson in how to get by in Hollywood. This was about how to get out. We're talking about the endgame here. Checkmate. What happens when the career begins to slide. It's a myth that when people in this town lose their viability, they long for some motion-picture relief home. This is Hollywood! There is no relief. No one leaves without a fight, and no one ever thinks he's too old. Even women executives in this town get erections. And by the way, let's not be fooled by those of us pretending to leave. No one is going anywhere. Everyone is fiercely gripping their balls, as I bet Jerry was now. For those of us who are really in bad shape, steeped in false sentimentality, we tend to burst into a river of tears when someone says, 'Whatever happened to Sydney Pollack?'

'I was just trying to point out that you don't seem to be the kinda hitmaker that makes the good old boys pleased to see you,' Jerry quickly added.

'Thanks.'

'Well, you're not exactly Jerry Bruckheimer, if you know what I mean.'

'What's your point?'

'No point.'

'Let's get serious. I produce, or I try to produce, *good* movies. Some work, some don't.'

'Whooey. Let's not talk about *good*. Let's talk about failure. This is a business. You ride in here trying to make money, and you get carried out if you don't. Who are you fooling?'

'Hey, I've produced some hits.'

'Oh, I believe it's been quite a while.'

'What kind of sinister shit is this? I came in here for breakfast, run into a bitter has-been . . .'

I hesitated. At least his frontal assault on my lack of success was more honest than the usual approach. Most times, within hours of the release of a movie that mercilessly tanks, your dearest Hollywood friends can't pass up the chance to ask, 'So how did your movie *do*?' Oh, they know how it did. They know the number. In fact, they know the number exactly. And they know its implications, but they can't resist watching you squirm at the news. At least Jerry's approach wasn't camouflaged with pity.

I was starting to wonder when my food would come.

'You're just pissed off because occasionally my phone rings and yours doesn't,' I said.

'Don't get so defensive. I was just trying to state the obvious. After all, it was you, I believe, who wrote, "In this town, three strikes and you're out."'

'Well, I was refering to . . .'

'You did say that, right?'

'But it was about . . .'

'If you'll allow me another sports metaphor, it might be time for you to CLEAN OUT YOUR LOCKER.' He actually started to laugh, almost uncontrollably.

That's it. I got up, gathered my papers. Fuck him. Hell, most in this town would have to wear paper bags with punched-out eyeholes to be seen sitting at a table with this guy. To be honest, if this weren't such an out-of-the-way café, I wouldn't be caught dead sitting here either. Jerry was one of the recently expunged. It's a common theme: with loss of power comes loss of libido. Stand next to it and you'll catch it.

'C'mon, sit . . . I have more to offer you than you think,' he said, wiping tears from his cheekbone.

'I don't think so. Call me touchy.'

'Really, we should talk about this. I mean, "Oh, I make *good* pictures," that's a good one. You need help.'

'Jerry, let's call it a day.'

'Please, I haven't talked to a real live producer in days. People aren't quite as happy to see me as they used to be.'

'It makes you wonder, doesn't it?'

You had to hand it to him, he wasn't running from his meteoric crash.

'Do you recall that movie where the little kid said he could see dead people, but they didn't always know they were dead?' Jerry was on a roll.

'Does that have some kinda personal implication, Jerry?'

'Let's just say that, sometimes after you've left the business, you can see through walls.'

My mood was darkening. 'Let's not start talkin' about corpses, Jerry, because I can already smell the rot.'

He gave me his biggest grin.

'I've become uninsultable.'

One of the few benefits of extinction, while all else crumbles, is the complete loss of vanity. The truth can no longer bite you in the ass.

Jerry had a point. Perhaps I had to take a hard look at those Fox years. I had produced a lot of movies, and – who was I kidding? – the overall results had been painful and often bloodstained. Maybe a thorough examination of the few small victories and the many vast defeats would not only reveal the process of making movies, but also explain the corkscrew smile I kept manufacturing at cocktail parties whenever someone said to me, 'Well, I, for one, don't care what anyone says, I *really liked Pushing Tin*.'

If I continued this messy exchange, I knew Jerry was going to get me to chew over those moments best left forgotten. He was going to revel in all of the gory details at my expense, and yet, call me a masochist, I was going to let him. In fact, I was getting inexorably drawn to the notion.

Times have certainly changed. Being a producer was never a bargain, but obsolescence was never expected. Had the producer turned into an emu?

The food finally arrived.

'Before we take this too far down the road, would you mind telling me what *bog stuffing* means?'

'*Snorkeling*, baby, bog *snorkeling*.' He then flicked his tongue in two quick, semicircular moves. No doubt about it, he was a beaut.

'Oh, dear lord' was all that I could whisper.

'What's the difference, what it means? You might not realize this now, kid, but this could be your lucky day.'

'I sorta felt that way the moment I saw you, Jerry.'

'Use me right and I can help you.'

'How so?'

'Suffice it to say, the end of the road for me could be a glimmer of hope for you . . . although, knowing you, I'm not so certain of that.'

'Last I checked, I was doin' just fine.'

'Look at your eyes; they've lost their confidence.'

'What exactly are we trying to get at here, Jerry?'

'I'm trying to get you to look at the last few years, really look, and maybe, just maybe, it will give you the grace to continue.'

He was turning into Mr. Rogers, and I was becoming Sally Field.

'You care. You really care,' I said without a shred of enthusiasm.

'I do care,' he said, his eyes almost moistening with concern.

'I get it . . . I get it. This isn't about me. You just want to hear the grim details. You're lonely and my failures comfort you. What to give a studio head has-been for Christmas? I know! Fill his stocking with the bitter memories of a producer tailspinning out of control. That'll keep him till Easter.'

'Actually, I can't deny a certain delicious pleasure from all of this. By the way, did you hear about the movie producer who got robbed and beaten on his front lawn by the Crips after he was followed home from Mr. Chow's?'

'Yes.'

'That's a good one.' He cackled with glee.

'Jerry, your heart is bigger than a bread box.'

Everyone, of course, knew about this incident, but only the most twisted were taking delight. I guess it just didn't get weird enough for Jerry. A few years back, he was devouring producers, writers, agents, like chum. Now, his only sustenance was to sit on the sideline and watch them burn. Most people preferred sports.

'I want to hear it all . . . slowly, please.' He was begging now.

'What's in it for me, again?'

'Let me count the ways: Hollywood salvation, a good throat-clearing, the will to go forward. Take your pick. I'm certain you will find it purging. It seems like a good bargain to me.'

He said this without his usual self-satisfied smirk. He was suddenly glowing with generosity and concern. Was he really interested? Not ole Jer. He used to be president of the Hollywood Venality Club. Could it be that the old warhorse wanted to shine a little light on those left behind?

'Jerry, let me get this straight. I get to delight you with all of the shit I've taken over the last few years, and your commiseration is going to make me feel good.'

'Yes.'

'You are one sick fuck.'

'Yes.'

'No.'

'Think colonoscopy. Believe you me, it's preventative. And besides, who else but me wants to hear it?'

He was vibrating now. The hook was in the water. He was having a terrific day.

'Just know, Jerry, if I were busy, I'd be gone.'

'I'm sure you would, but you're not and I'm not. I want to hear it all. What was that first picture you did at Fox? *Great Expectations*! Let's go torture another classic. Oh, boy . . . who can we cornhole after we're finished with Dickens? Or was it that "bear" thing that Mamet wrote? Was that the first picture? Oh, yeah, Alec Baldwin. I bet he's a lot of fun. Loves producers, I hear. Hoo ha.'

The vein on the left side of his neck was pumping. He was known in the backrooms of Hollywood as the ultimate swine and there was no stopping him now.

'And how about that seventies rock movie? What was it called? *Go Go Bliss* or something like that.'

'It was called *Sunset Strip*.'

'What the hell was that? As I recall, Fox opened it in only one theater. How about that. One theater! A baby-killing! What a massacre that must have been. Your idea, was it?'

'I'm afraid so.'

'Fuck me . . . and they still let you continue after that? Please, save that barbarous tale for last. What visionaries those Fox execs must have been. Real high-watt bulbs, there. You must love those guys. Oh . . . wait . . . I almost forgot . . . *Fight Club. Fight Club.* Woowee . . . Good God, man, you really like to make people feel warm and fuzzy, don't ya?'

He was certainly prepared. You had to give him that.

This was going to take more than a breakfast.

TWO

TWO GUYS AND A BEAR

'Hi, this is Bill Mechanic.' The call came directly – no secretary. He was the new film production head at Fox. Dialing the phone all by himself, I thought, was rather casual and rare. In Hollywood, when you were on my side of the mattress, a little bit of generosity went a long way, especially if you wanted to kiss on the first date.

'Hi, Bill, howsit going?'

'I'm well. Listen, I'm in Palm Springs now, but when I return, I think we should get together.' He spoke matter-of-factly, almost as if we had met or talked before.

The truth is we only knew each other from press releases in the trades. I knew that he just got the new big plum job at Fox, having been wooed over from Disney by Peter Chernin, and he knew that I was at the tail end of a contract at Warner Bros., where I had just put out the artistically interesting but dismally unsuccessful *This Boy's Life*. I remember that when it was first test-screened in a Pasadena multiplex, Terry Semel, the then graceful but remote head of Warners, walked up to me at the concession stand, dressed in the newest Armani casual, looked me square in the eye, and slowly nodded.

'It's a *good* movie and that's *all* that's important,' he said in a calm and reassuring voice.

'Well, thanks so much, Terry, it is a *good* movie, isn't it?'

'It's hard to make a *good* movie.'

'Very.'

At previews, everyone spoke euphemistically. I was fucked.

I knew too well that at that very moment Terry's entire distribution staff was in the back alley throwing up on their shoes. You could almost hear them through the crack in the men's room door: 'Oh, mother of Christ, De Niro is in this dining room kicking the living piss out of sweet little Leonardo DiCaprio . . . how the fuck are we going to sell this shit!' 'I know! How 'bout selling it as *Father Knows Best* for the criminally insane?!' 'Dead beavers and pedophilia, what are they gonna let those disturbed assholes do next?!!' You get the picture. *Good* in Hollywood is a euphemism for 'grease up, bite the belt, and try not squeal too much when this baby comes out.' Well, I tried not to squeal, but I can't say it bolstered my confidence any. Let's just say the call from Mechanic came at a very good time.

'Lookin' forward to it, Bill.' I couldn't have been friendlier.

It was several weeks before I heard from Bill again, but during that time I had started to work with Michael Mann on what would eventually become *Heat*. It was the early stages. Michael was reworking a script that he had written several years earlier and had actually produced and directed for ABC television under a different title, *L.A. Takedown*. No writer likes to throw anything away. So with a fresh rewrite, we had hoped to attract De Niro and Pacino and expand the story into a much larger movie. Since Michael had already told the same story once before, his only option was to try to make this one bigger, and hopefully better.

I was entering my final year at Warners, and the likelihood of them renewing my contract after *This Boy's Life* was extremely remote. Since it would be at least eighteen months before *Heat* could be released, assuming that it would even get made – something you can never count on in Hollywood – my contract would have long since expired. On the lot, I was viewed as a man slowly dying of a disease that might be contagious. If you were listening, there were always clues.

'So, what's goin' on for you next year?' Bruce Berman, then head of film production under Semel and a man not well known for sticking his neck out, would subtly ask.

'Gee whiz, Bruce, I'm thinking of taking up fishing, how 'bout you?'

'You know what I mean. What's the five-year plan?'

Since I had only ten months left, I knew where this conversation was going. Bruce was a crafty insider. He could take the temperature of the town. I think he was trying to help.

'Ya know, you producers have the toughest jobs in town,' he continued.

'I'll say.'

'Boy, I can't tell you what utter respect I have for it.'

'Really.'

'Requires real fortitude to be a self-starter.'

'Bruce, you're making me cry.'

'Always flying sans parachute. No safety net.'

'I thought a contract was a safety net.'

'Those deals are getting passé, too costly. Might as well read it in the trades – they're dryin' up.'

'Is this a trend or a phase?' I queried.

'Let's just say it's a good time to be an *executive*.'

I asked Bruce about the other producing deals on the lot. I couldn't help myself.

'What about Jerry Weintraub? He's still here.'

'Oh, he's very close with the Bush family.'

'George Bush!'

'Get a grip, pal.'

'And Joel Silver?' I asked, but I knew he was a long-time permanent fixture.

'Oh, c'mon, my man, he's off buying furniture with Jane [Semel].'

I was going to need a job.

My first meeting with Bill was at the Fox commissary. Since I hadn't been to Fox since Dick Zanuck was running the place years ago, I was looking forward to driving through 'the front gate' and getting that little buzz one gets when first entering a movie lot. After a cumbersome ten-minute hassle waiting for the guard to find the 'drive-on pass' (the days of 'How nice to see you Mr. L., please drive right through' were long gone), I was allowed to park in a new parking structure about one quarter mile from the commissary. Call it a buildup of years and layers of cynicism, but there was no buzz. As I was rushing through the parking structure and down the walkway to the commissary, not wanting to be late for the initial meet, something felt off. The place, for me, had lost its allure. The vibe was gone. The new corporate head-quarters being built across from the *NYPD Blue* set was jutting skyward with foreboding glass and steel sides and a witless entry sculpture – some giant black ball spinning in water. It had an architectural intention that said the past is dead, California is dead, the foreign takeover is almost complete.

I guess the obvious target in all this is Rupert Murdoch, who, after all, had bought the place and if he wished had the right to turn Fox into a used-car lot. Blaming Murdoch alone, however, would be too easy. The lot's new look was a sign of the corporate times. But this was about more than looks. Efficiency because of rising costs had replaced inspiration. There were too many lawyers, too many marketing stiffs, and not enough creative types for this kind of dream machinery to work. For the people who make the stuff, it was a dangerous sign. A bad mix. It might have been my mood, but for me a delicate dance step had clearly been violated at Fox. It didn't bode well for greatness or success.

The commissary was even worse. The overlit dining room had a flat, used smell. Bad colors, shitty wallpaper. It had become institutional. The waiters with pale neoned complexions were mechanically stalking the room. As I was being led to a table in the rear, I recognized Murdoch, sitting with two 'suits,' making private phone calls while occasionally glaring across the room. He was imperious. So what? Imperiousness was benchmark behavior for studio owners. It was assumed, a familiar pattern where the guy at the top and his minions were oceans apart. With the invisible ax always inches from their heads, they withheld their disdain with obsequious smiles. But this wasn't anything new. What was new, with the rise of corporate vertical integration, was that the guy at the top – in this case Murdoch – didn't care about movies any more than he cared about baseball. Owning Fox's motion picture business was merely a required charm on the mega-media-conglomerate bracelet. A necessary evil. An essential irritant that economically didn't pencil out. I wondered if the food was going to match the atmosphere.

If you're asking, with all of my split-second dire observations, why I didn't call for my car and head for the front gate, the answer was simple: *money*.

Mechanic was already seated, three tables away from Rupert. As I approached him, I ran into the venerable Fox producer Larry Gordon. I knew, he knew, and everyone in the street knew that he was soon to be on the way out. But, what was interesting about Larry was his ability to maintain a bemused defiance in the face of some of the most horrific setbacks that a producer can confront. He'd had some past successes, but his recent losses were piling up like New York garbage. I respected his indomitability, but his lunch gave him away. All he was eating was a dry baked potato with salsa.

'Hey, Larry, I guess you didn't care for the special, huh?' I asked.

'No fats,' he replied. 'I'm going light these days.'

'Why so?'

'Bad heart. Can't tolerate fats.' He shrugged with a wave and a breezy smile. Underneath the charm, his digestive system and his arteries had paid a wearisome price.

I knew that when he saw me with Mechanic, he would quickly assume I was being lured over to Fox. But did he know that I was to get *his* offices after he was tossed? And so it goes.

'Really nice to see you, Larry,' I said.

'Yeah, really nice.'

As I neared Bill's table, he stood and we shook hands. My first take on Bill was that I liked him. He was rounder than your typical executive, which gave him a more available, less threatening demeanor. His shirt was too dark to be corporately correct, his tie was all wrong, his shoes were strange, very strange, actually. I found out later that he was an animal rights activist and a strict vegetarian, so naturally, his shoes were made of Naugahyde with rubber soles and his car upholstery was made of cloth. He might have to skin an agent now and again, but I suppose the cows were safe.

We both ordered veggie burgers. As we began the compulsory small talk, I noticed that the *computer* word kept popping up. Bill liked to talk numbers: grosses, preview scores, ratios of scripts to movies made, ratios of movies made to hits made, etc. He also liked to talk about movies in the past that excited him. He seemed to care about movies, and he even seemed to *like* the people who made the movies – an oxymoron for an executive in this day. It was too early to make any assumptions, but I was hoping that his gut rather than his bean-counting was going to play the major role in his decision-making. I wasn't concerned. After all, if the computer hadn't spilled out some past hits under my name, Mechanic and I wouldn't be having this lunch.

As I glanced over Bill's shoulder, I accidentally made eye contact with Murdoch. I felt the chill. He didn't know who I was, but his look reflected grave disappointment, as if he foretold the next few years. It was either disappointment or gas from the dreadful commissary food. In any case, I was certain that Rupert and Bill did not come from the same block. Maybe I was getting suckered, but Bill seemed like a bona fide movie fan. Murdoch was not projecting the same colors. A fishy blend, if you asked me. Had Rupert actually interviewed Mechanic before he got the job? Were their corporate goals shared? I had to wonder: When this drama finally played out (as do all executive dramas in Hollywood), would Bill be left with any of his vital organs? Get a pathologist. Murdoch ate meat.

'I'm lookin' to sign a couple of producers to help supply us with movies over the next few years. Would you be interested?' Bill was simple and direct.

'Yes,' I said, even more directly.

I explained that I could start after my Warners contract ended. Since *Heat* was still in the early planning stages for Warners and none of us knew what a sizable hit it was going to be, it was apparent to me that Warners would be only too happy to let me sign elsewhere. If they let me out of my contract early, they could save some money.

And now for the hard question.

'What kind of movies are you thinking of producing?' he asked. 'I'm sure you have something up your sleeve.'

'Shit, Bill, I haven't given it much thought. I'm working with Michael Mann on this thing for Warners, and after that . . . I think, uh, I'm going to develop something with, uh, David Mamet . . . and then maybe a kind of a Dickens sorta thing.'

'Really, what?'

'It's all still in the planning stages.' I didn't have a clue.

'Sounds good. Let me have our lawyers get this started and see if we can make a deal.'

'Thanks.'

'We're lookin' forward to it.'

'Me too.'

'By the way . . .'

'Huh?'

'. . . you could use a hit.'

'I know.' I couldn't help but glance over at Murdoch, who for a millisecond glared back with a 'Who the fuck are you?' look. I should have made a run for it.

'Well, let's just hope it's for us.' Bill smiled.

'Here's hoping,' I said lightly, mustering up my finest acting. Dodging direct eye contact with Bill or Murdoch, I turned to look for Larry Gordon. He was gone.

'Oooh, man, he gave you the "You could use a hit," shot, did he? I like him.'

'Thought you'd enjoy that, Jerry.'

'That'll freeze the testicles.'

' 'Fraid so.'

'Where was that slippery Chernin [the News Corp executive just below Murdoch and just above Mechanic] in all this?'

'He would hover and come in and out when it was convenient.'

'Makes you thinka bacon grease, dunnit?'

'I haven't given that part much thought yet, Jerry. Why don't we try to stick to a syntax we both understand?'

'Looks to me like Mechanic was sandwiched and you were the cheap brown bag carrying the lunch.'

'I think we're getting a little ahead of ourselves, don't you?'

'You're right, you're right. Go slow, I want details.'

There we were at a new restaurant. Jerry wanted to meet at the

Ivy at the Shore for lunch, an upscale hangout in Santa Monica but thankfully not as visible as the Grill in Beverly Hills. I suppose it's of little value to describe what Jerry was wearing, but there was something about tri-striped, blue Adidas running pants, Gucci slippers, and a very old Ferrari sweatshirt on a desperate middle-aged man that must be looked at, particularly when it occurred to me that the same stuff was neatly folded in my own drawers. Were we turning 'casual' Friday into 'sweaty casual' Friday? Since our breakfast in Malibu, his tan had faded, but the promise of tasting a little Hollywood action had apparently given him a boost.

No need to ask why I'd decided to continue this dialogue. I'm aware that I must have been deeply disturbed to let Jerry beat the shit out of me again as we painfully traveled down memory lane. I had some serious issues to work out. I kept justifying to myself that when the future looks hazy and dark, who better to talk to then someone who had a big past and no future? Who else would have a better feel for desperation than Jerry? My consolation: No matter how bitter he became, I always knew he was drowning faster than me. I had no idea then that he had a firm grip on my pant leg.

'Two chopped-vegetable salads,' the waiter politely interrupted. 'Who gets the one with shrimp, no chicken, no oil in the dressing, asparagus instead of egg, no avocado, balsamic vinegar on the side?'

'Me.' I raised my hand, noticing that ordering a salad was getting as complicated as selecting a coffee at Starbucks.

'Oh, gosh, welcome back, sir.' The waiter blanched, then genuflected, when he realized that was *the* Jerry. 'It's been years, sir, hasn't it?' The waiter's expression of doubt mixed with awe said it all. He assumed that Jerry was 'dead', but just in case Jerry could spin some kind of showbiz voodoo reincarnation and actually make a comeback, a little anal massage couldn't hurt. Everyone in town was in on this game.

'Well, thank you, Jeff. Did you ever finish that screenplay?' Jerry's question was generic. It didn't require an answer. Who wasn't finishing a script in this place? It was as meaningless as asking about one's health or the weather.

'As a matter of fact, sir, we're this far [thumb and forefinger almost touching] from a start date.'

'Well, isn't that just great,' Jerry said, trying to camouflage his annoyance that any good news brought.

'And do you know what else?' Jeff was grinning now.

'What?'

'I'm going to direct.'

'Direct?' Jerry had had enough.

'Direct.'

'Oh, how special.'

'Nice to see you out again, sir, enjoy your lunch,' Jeff added over his shoulder on his way to the kitchen.

Jerry sat there for a moment, not ready to reach for his food. He was conflicted. Jeff's enthusiasms rankled his spirit. You could see the bubble over his head – 'Even the fuckin' waiter's got some Hollywood love.'

Nonetheless, being acknowledged again, even by a food server, was like giving blood to a vampire. His mood was tempered.

'Hey, you know that "bear" movie you did?'

'Yes. My first venture at Fox.'

'Word has it that Alec Baldwin carved some new assholes for you and that director of yours.'

'Not exactly true . . . and anyways, that story has to start at the beginning.'

'Why not cut to the grim bits and leave out the boring stuff?'

'Jerry, it's my dime, it's my therapy. You're gonna have to listen to the whole story if I'm gonna let you get off on the bad parts.'

'You're right, and anyways, where am I going? . . . After all [his

22

thumb and forefinger almost touching], I'm *this far* from a start date,'
he bellowed, bursting into a laugh.

'*This far!*' I replied.

In a brief moment of bonding, I held up my thumb and forefinger
and we tapped hands in a drinkless toast.

'Okay, back to business, how did that car wreck of a "bear" movie
happen?' Jerry asked.

'It wasn't a car wreck.'

'Not what I heard.'

In the basement of the Fox administration building, just below Bill
Mechanic's and Peter Chernin's offices, were two screening rooms:
the Z room and the S room. They were built in the old Darryl
Zanuck days, circa 1940. According to legend, and who cares if it's
true or not, Zanuck, ensconced in room Z, would spend countless
nights with his masseuse and assorted girls reviewing dailies,
examining rough cuts, and doing whatever else that was handy.
No one but Zanuck was allowed to use it. His florid excesses were
legendary. The S room, apparently lettered after Joseph Schenck,
was for the general use of other executives. Although Zanuck was
responsible for the supervision of thirty-five pictures a year, he mixed
business with pleasure and still maintained a healthy list of enemies.
Today, the chance of interrupting an executive in mid-blow-job at
three in the morning, while dailies are being screened, is over. That
kind of action is reserved for pols or dot.com guys. Hollywood has
gone corporate and square. You don't have to worry about knocking
anymore.

'Are you sure all I have to say is "it's two guys and a bear, they get
lost in the forest and have to learn to survive together even though
one guy was trying to kill the other guy and take his young, beautiful
wife"?' David Mamet asked.

He was not particularly concerned. He just wanted some reassurance that I had already worked things out and that this was going to be a mere formality. He had that look of 'I'll do my job, did you do yours?'

'Yep, it's in the bag,' I said.

We were making the long walk down the wide administration building hallway, the wallpaper still revealing some leftover touches of Zanuck Green (a color that Zanuck insisted on because it matched his mother's nail polish), to deliver a pitch to Tom Jacobson, the newly appointed head of film production under Bill Mechanic. Wait a minute! Who's Tom Jacobson? Wasn't Mechanic the newly appointed head of film production under Chernin? And wasn't Chernin, who dutifully reported to Murdoch, head of worldwide motion pictures? Well, yes, it's all true. It's a complicated system. Even the most experienced insider has a gruesome time trying to find out *where the buck stops*. If you're looking for solid answers, it's rare to find them in movie meetings.

The best way an outsider can understand these subtle distinctions is by asking who has the power to say yes, maybe, or no. Tom Jacobson could say no, but if he wanted to say yes to anything, he would have to appeal to Bill Mechanic for an approval. And even if he wanted to say no, Mechanic could overrule him, assuming you knew how to get to Mechanic. If this request was very expensive, such as the green-lighting of a fifty-million-dollar movie, Mechanic would have to appeal to Chernin for approval. If Mechanic wanted to say no, it would end there, unless you could appeal to Chernin to overrule Mechanic. If a request was very, very expensive, such as more money for a *Titanic* production that was running mercilessly out of control, Chernin would have to ask Murdoch for approval. As complicated as all this seems, it is a layered committee method designed to pass on the risks and defuse the blame. As you might suspect, the executive at the bottom of this pole is naked. Daryl Hannah's manager wields more power. This guy might be able to jaw his way into a good table at a restaurant with his Fox film production presidential business card, but when he went to work the next day, he was a duck waiting to hear the gunshot.

Tom Jacobson had *that* job.

I had called David six weeks before. After several months of negotiations, my exclusive deal with Fox to produce movies for them over the next three years had been completed. It was nice to have the deal, but I needed to get something going – to put some scripts in development and kick-start the promises. The first rule of producing is to find a writer with an idea, or to get an idea and find a writer. Making friends with agents can be handy, but it's way down the food chain. Since David and I did *The Untouchables* together, we had developed a good professional working relationship: *You get me a lot of money, I get you a good script.* I was hoping that if I leaned on David, he could pull some rabbit out of the hat. His price to write a screenplay had skyrocketed. I knew this rabbit would be costly.

I placed the call.

'Hi, Dave.'

'What's the shot?'

'I got a new deal, I'm lookin for you to write a new script.'

'Fine.'

'There'll be lots of money.'

'Good. Let's do it.'

'It's not that easy.'

'Why?'

'Because if you don't tell me what it's about, I can't get you the money.'

'Fine. What do you want it to be about?'

'I don't know; that's why I'm calling you.'

'I understand.'

'Dave, how about an adventure movie?'

'Fine.'

'Something castable. Two guys, maybe.'

'Fine.'

'C'mon, Dave, I need more to go on.'

'Okay . . . how 'bout two guys and a bear.'

'It's a start.'

'That's all I got.'

'I need more.'

'I'll get back to you.'

'Thank you.'

Within a short time he did get back to me with a rather well-worked-out wilderness story that promised big intrigue, a fierce struggle for survival, betrayal, and of course, a bear. I was quite confident that Fox would be engaged, but it was early in the process. Even if they agreed to the screenplay, there was no assurance that it would be made into a movie. We were still smarting over our last venture together at Warner Bros. He had written *Ordinary Daylight*, a powerful script based on a true story written by Andrew Potok about his struggle with retinitis pigmentosa. Much money was spent, many meetings with directors and executives were taken, but the movie was never made. We were preempted by Al Pacino's *Scent of a Woman*. In the end, Warners balked.

'How can we make a movie about a guy who's going blind but doesn't get better?'

'We thought you knew that. It's in the book!'

'Pacino's blind in his movie but he can drive a Ferrari and dance for God's sake.'

'Didn't anyone read the book?' I appealed.

'Of course, we assumed you were going to fix those bits.'

'But it's a true story!'

'Who gives a shit if it's a true story?'

And so on. Suffice it to say it was another wonderful Mamet script, at least that's my take, that never got made. The consolation prize is that he got paid a shitload of money. But for the producer, when a movie doesn't get made, there is nothing to show for the time and the ultimate defeat. Moreover, the failed results usually reveal the importance of getting everyone on the same railroad track before the script is ever read. When the buyer doesn't get what he thinks he bought, it is because miscommunications exist before one word is written. These discrepencies start to occur as soon as the first question is asked: *So what's the idea?* at the pitch meeting.

I assured Mamet that this meeting was merely academic. I had already explained to Mechanic the general drift of the idea, but he had insisted for purposes of protocol that we run it past Jacobson. Could we do it on the phone? I asked. No. Proper protocol, he insisted, meant going to Jacobson's office. Since Mamet lived in Boston, this required a trip to LA, which always left him in a mixed mood. A trip to LA may seem like a small price to pay to pick up one-million-plus dollars, but pitching is pitching. At its best, even when it's operating on all cylinders, it's annoying. At its worst, it's a humiliation for everyone in the room.

Halfway down the hallway, getting ever closer to Jacobson's office, we slowed down to look at the *Three Faces of Eve* poster.

'Can you believe this studio made that movie? Gosh, what has happened to this place?' I asked.

'Time mixed with cowardice,' Mamet said.

'You're right, you're always right.'

'This is not going to be one of those meetings where we walk in and no one knows why we are there?'

'Please. I'm a professional.'

We stopped to glance at the *Alien* poster.

'So, I say the usual, right?'

'The usual,' I said.

'It's a cross between *Raiders of the Lost Ark* and *Wuthering Heights*.'

'That's right.'

As we entered the office of Tom Jacobson, the first thing that screamed out was that there were two secretarial desks. This guy must be very busy. Mechanic, his boss, had only one secretary.

'Mr. Jacobson is off the phone now, he's ready to see you.'

'Thank you.'

For those of you who have never been in a pitch meeting, it's nothing much different from door-to-door sales except the financial stakes are higher. You must convince the guy with the checkbook that he *needs* whatever soap you are selling. I'm not sure anyone actually *needs* to buy an idea for a movie. If you buy an idea, you have to pay to have the script written. Writers are expensive. In most instances the scripts are badly done and only a small percentage ever get filmed. Because of the high turnover factor, the executive who winds up buying the script probably won't even have his job by the time the wretched thing gets made and is ready for release. Either someone else will be the beneficiary of its success, or the poor sucker who was fired will inevitably be blamed for supporting it. Under these rules, I'm always amazed at the optimism that's displayed so early on for something that might not pay off for years. Nonetheless, this is the very start of the process, and decisions made at this level have enormous impact.

We entered Tom's office accompanied by his assistant. It turned out to be twice the size of Mechanic's office. Hmmm. I didn't step it off, but I was tempted. If my office were twice the size of that of the guy who hired me, I would immediately ask for some partitions or at the very least donate a good part of it to some dispossessed underling. 'Oh, please, Bill, this office is too big. All's I need is a desk, a phone, and two chairs – why don't *you* take my grand office?' Being offered all of this grandness smelled like a setup to me. Call me cynical, but it sure felt as if this guy, whom we were about to meet, were renting. I didn't know then that his lease was only month to month.

'Boston's a wonderful city,' Tom said as he leaned back in his chair, his feet pushing back from the coffee table.

'Sure is.'

'Cultural.'

'Very.'

'Gosh, I love it, the seasons you know.'

'Uh-huh.'

'Winter,' Tom said, trying to make out Mamet's reaction.

Awkward silence.

'You like sports?' Tom politely continued, trying to keep this ship afloat.

'Not that interested.'

The room was dying.

Tom turned his attention toward me. 'So, we know what David's been up to, what about you?'

'Well, I'm at Fox working for you.'

Awkward silence.

Tom was encouraging me to get this fucker rolling. Even Mamet was looking at me peculiarly as if to say, 'What exactly do *you* do for a living?'

I took the hint.

'Well, Tom, Dave here has this good idea for a movie.'

Tom, who was a mellow, diminutive sort, gave me a glance of 'thanks for the help.' Everyone's patience was shaky. Introductory small talk at pitch meetings, especially when the parties are complete strangers, always disintegrates into a gooey, treacly mess. Tom put his fingertips together and placed them near his lips.

'So, c'n you tell me a little bit of what's it about?'

'Indeed, I can.' David starts in speaking at a rapid pace. 'There's this extremely wealthy and refined bookish man living in New York who is married and very much in love with a beautiful, young fashion model, who has an assignment to go on a photo shoot in the wilds of Alaska.

The photographer, a dashing young up-and-comer, who will be doing the shoot knows the girl. She invites her husband to go – a get-outta-the-house sort of thing. We soon learn that there is some competition between the two men for the girl. In fact, the photographer has an agenda to maybe do away with our bookish gentleman, marry the model, and inherit the wealth. And our girl may be in on it. Before he gets a chance, however, the two men, while sightseeing for locations in a small plane, violently crash in the middle of no—'

'Could I stop you there for a second.' Tom jumps in with an uneasy look on his face. David was just revving up.

'Am I going too fast?'

'No . . . it's not that . . .'

'Is the setup clear?'

'I'm following you all right . . .'

'Perhaps I should start over.'

'No, not necessary.'

'Well, what's the problem?'

'I just wonder if the smart fellow has to have so much money?'

'Huh?'

'You know, I'm worried.'

'You're worried?'

'I'm concerned, that's all.'

Mamet shoots me a 'Where do we go from here?' glare.

'But they're trying to get his money,' I chime in, hoping David will stay in his seat.

'I know.'

'If he has no money, then there's no sense in trying to get it, that's the plot,' I said, almost begging.

'Okay then, let me ask *you*, David, do *you* really think an audience can root for a guy who has money?'

David waits for several seconds as if he were just asked to explain the concept of time in the universe.

'Yes.'

For some reason this detour threw David and everyone else in the room into the wrong spin. The rhythm of the pitch had been inexorably altered. David's spirit had darkened. Where were we? Should he start over? What were the rules? Finally, Tom took charge.

'All right then . . . let's continue.'

'Um, well, then they run into a bear,' David said quietly, '. . . and then they kill the bear.' It was all that he could muster.

After a long, clumsy pause, we all stood up. Tom thanked us and said he would get back to us as soon as possible. In Jacobson's defense, one of the job descriptions of a film executive, I suppose, is to be mindful of what the audience wants. Unfortunately, no one except Jerry Bruckheimer seems to know what that is.

In the hallway I couldn't help but notice the poster of *The Poseidon Adventure* as we made our brisk walk through the building. The ad line at the top read, 'Hell, Upside Down,' while a giant crashing tidal wave was about to drown a cast of thousands.

'What just happened?' David asked.

'I think it went well.'

'What's it like when it goes bad?'

'They tell you *no* in the room.'

Remnants of six freshly baked chocolate chip cookies, an Ivy at the Shore specialty, were scattered next to the bill. Jerry looked at me with a semisatisfied smirk. He knew I was going to pay. The accepted protocol in this town was that the one still functioning was the one who paid. There's a pecking order to all this. Agents always pay. Executives usually pay. Talent never pays. And producers rarely get asked out. For those who have left the business, voluntarily or not, the courtesy was for the survivor to pick up the tab. And a show of gratitude was never required since the assumption was that those who were still working had an expense account. It wasn't really their money anyway. And besides, Jerry wasn't large on gratitude.

'Frankly, this story is very dull,' Jerry proclaimed.

'Why?'

'No drama.'

'How so?'

'This deal had to make.'

'I wasn't so sure.'

'If Mamet were drooling all over his shoes and said, "I want to write about the art of grilling squid," you woulda ended up with a deal.'

'Jerry, I think you've been out of the loop for too long.'

'Please, you were in your honeymoon phase, it was a no-brainer. Or as Dawn Steel used to say, "Hello!" '

'I don't take anything for granted.'

'Once Mechanic spent all this money on you, what's he gonna do on the first thing you're excited about? Say, "Fuck you!" I think not. Wait'll you deliver a coupla stink bombs his way. Wait'll one of those beauties of yours gets made and opens on a Friday and you get the death call on Monday. You'll see, Mamet's gonna have to sound like Richard Burton in a tutu reciting Macbeth before you're gonna get the cash.'

'Don't hold back.'

Of course, Jerry was being astute. There is a grace period where the buyer wants to believe he's made the right purchase. Mechanic had just made this deal with me. He's got to show some support or his superior is going to question why the hell the deal was made in the first place.

'Y'know, I really miss sitting in on those pitch meetings,' Jerry said wistfully. 'If you'll permit me a movie metaphor, "Aahh . . . it's like the fresh smell of napalm in the morning" . . . I was good at it. I would listen patiently, with my eyes slightly moist, waiting for the person to finish his or her ambitious tale. Then, I would lean back with a complicit nod to show artistic respect. And then, after the room went still for about ten seconds, I would draw an appreciative smile, letting them see my soft side, and say, "It's just not my cup of wonton. Sorry." Ooohweee . . . like a cool breeze in summer.'

'Jerry, that's why you're loved.'

THREE

OVER THE EDGE

I t w a s t h e middle of December and I was feeling smug. It was one of those good Hollywood mornings where I actually woke up with the confidence that I'm usually faking. This was due to a combination of things. A morning article in the trades had surfaced, revealing that Paramount's most profitable movie of the year was *Clueless*, a light comedy written and directed by Amy Heckerling, whose first movie, *Fast Times at Ridgemont High*, had been produced by me ages ago. It wasn't simply the parental pride that gave me the satisfying glow. The mention that *Clueless* had been developed by Fox and subsequently put into turnaround by Fox was the intriguing sidebar. This meant that after the executives Jacobson, Mechanic, and Chernin et al. had read the script, they'd passed on it. For myriad of reasons they collectively believed that it was too silly, wouldn't work, and it was time to recoup some development costs. So they had quickly sold it off to Scott Rudin and Paramount, only to get snakebitten by its success months later. While Paramount was celebrating their most profitable movie of that year, Fox was languishing in last place in total yearly grosses among all of the major studios.

One can only imagine Murdoch receiving the good news, baseball bat resting quietly in his hand, putting on his best Capone/De Niro/Mamet rhythms: 'What!? What, am I alone in this world or are we a team . . . blah blah blah,' before restraining himself from turning someone's head into grapefruit.

These kinds of mistakes, particularly when they are in the press, always give the executives at any studio a jolt of insecurity, reconfirming their deeply hidden fears that maybe they don't have a fucking clue. Before they can regain their confidence (and it doesn't take them long), the next bunch of salesmen through the door get the benefit of the doubt. When a studio is weak, opportunities are created. When agents and producers start marching up and down the hallways saying, 'Don't worry, I'm a doctor, stand aside, I know what I'm doing,' for a brief period they will be endorsed.

Good timing was veering in my direction. I had two scripts ready to be made: *Great Expectations*, a meat-cleaving experience that I will get into later, and *Bookworm*, the newly completed Mamet script. I was searching for a director and a cast for each movie, and more important, I was trying to convince the powers that be at Fox to spend money. A lot of money. 'C'mon, gentlemen, "two guys and a bear," lust, violence, courage under fire, can't miss with this one, let's make it!'

The second boost for me was that *Heat* was about to be premiered at the Steven J. Ross theater on the Warners lot. The buzz for the movie was soaring. De Niro and Pacino facing each other off in a movie for the first time (you can't count *Godfather II* because they were never together in the same scene) was having an enormous impact. After a year and a half and more than a few battles, Michael Mann had finally made the movie that he'd always wanted to make out of this material. Unwittingly, I couldn't help but feel that my stock was rising. My step was lighter. I was acting like *them*. I would attend meetings at Fox and the look on my face said it all: 'You're all a bunch of dumb fucks, listen ta me and I'll lead you outta this horrible mess you all got yourselves into.'

A producer bursting with confidence can be a truly ugly sight.

The only hitch (and at this point a minor hitch) was that Tom Jacobson, the guy who had heard the pitch from Mamet months before, had 'stepped down' from his position at Fox to return to a more 'hands-on moviemaking role.' At least that's what the announcement in *Variety* declared. This is Hollywood-speak that means he got ceremoniously dumped by his superiors and was forced to forge onward as a movie producer. No one wants that. I guess someone had to fall for past disappointments, and it sure wasn't going to be Chernin or Mechanic, at least, not yet. Frankly, I was disappointed. After that wacky pitch meeting, Jacobson and I had found a reasonable way to work with each other. Since you never knew whom they were going to bring out of the dugout, the abrupt change in command meant I would have to start the inconvenient executive-bonding dance all over again. You remember what Stephen Stills said: 'If you can't be with the one you love, love the one you're with.'

Tom Jacobson was replaced by a gangly lawyer, Tom Rothman, who had previously been running the Fox Searchlight division for about six months. Before becoming an executive he had had a short and rather empty stint as a movie producer. He couldn't make a go of it. Our first encounter was chilly. He talked, I listened. He conducted the entire meeting with his back to me while he was organizing some papers behind his computer. I suppose he was either showing me that he could do more than one thing at a time or else he was saying, 'Since I couldn't make a go of it as a producer, fuck you for trying.'

Let's just say for now that Rothman, after receiving his new promotion, was short on humility. He did not share this disease alone. After all, when you get 'chosen,' you contract the same virus that everyone else gets in Hollywood when presented with some power. You think you *know*. Before the marketplace gets the chance to punish you, really punish you, you actually believe you're onto something. You know what works. You were born with it. Within a short time, however, you're hopelessly bedridden, just praying that one of the giant directors will come along and revive *Planet of the Apes 4* or *Star Wars 6* or *Terminator 3* and save your sorry ass. If that doesn't work, you're on the phone with Robin Williams's agent begging him to get Robin to put the multiflowered dress back on and play an older woman one more time. Once one of those tent poles gets released, Rothman and his ilk will be front and center, crowing about their newfound legacy, the legacy they had nothing to with, hoping not to be found out. Murdoch has shown a knack for seeing through that charade.

Early proclamations of making pictures with integrity, support for new directors, or the need to be progressive soon fades like cheap designer jeans. It is more than just an exhaustion of fresh ideas; it is the sticky fear of taking a risk. In less than a year, the executive's appetite to be a pioneer is replaced by the desperation to hold on to an overpriced job – hold on, no matter what. Fortunately, since Mechanic and Chernin were still running the show, Rothman's early pontifications proved to be an annoying but minor inconvenience.

For me, I had to get a cast and secure a director, or *Bookworm* wasn't going to get made.

'Do you know why you are rapidly losing the hair on your ankles?' Dustin Hoffman asked me, noticing I was not wearing socks.

'No. Not really,' I said, glancing at my feet.

'You're getting older.'

'Oh.'

'It's a genetic thing.'

'Interesting.'

'Loss of testosterone, really.'

'I see.'

'It doesn't happen to everyone.'

'Can something be done?'

'I'm afraid not.'

'Nothing?'

'I don't think so.'

I looked over at Lee Tamahori, wondering if he knew how to shift the focus of the conversation. We were entering into the second hour of our meeting with Dustin, and we still hadn't gotten to the script. Lee returned the look as if to say, 'Is this how you guys do it up here?' Preliminary small talk was taking on a new meaning.

Lee, a Kiwi, had recently directed his first movie, *Once Were Warriors*, a spirited tale of a Maori family dealing with contemporary life in urban New Zealand. This spirited, raw, hard-edged movie with an emotionally aching core had become the highest-grossing film in New Zealand's history. After seeing the movie, I sent *Bookworm* to Lee and was buoyed by his interest. The studio, because of the sizzle that *Once Were Warriors* had created, was cautiously encouraging us to get a couple of 'stars'; only then, they implied, would they fund the movie. No guarantees, but so far so good.

We met with Mechanic and Jacobson to make cast lists. Jacobson could not, at the time, have known that the guillotine was inches from his neck, the lever having already been pulled. We were there to ask: Who were the key actors who could play an aging, wealthy bookworm? Who were the key actors who could play a younger fashion photographer intent on stealing the bookworm's money and wife? These lists did not necessarily include the 'best' actor for the job. For example, Robert Duvall may be a brilliant casting choice for the bookworm, but when the computer tallies up his recent box office wreckage, he may not be considered as good a business choice as Bill Cosby. Trying to create a pecking order that would satisfy us as well as the studio turned into a random guessing game. Which actor, if he could play the role, would sell the most tickets? Who knows? Who can ever know? Certainly not us. We were rats chasing our tails.

First, we received the obligatory and expected turndown from Harrison Ford. At that time, any script written that required a male lead over forty-five went directly to Harrison because his acquiescence ensured a start date. It wouldn't matter if the character was an international spy or a transvestite. If the character was an older male, it went to Ford; unless, of course, Tom Cruise was interested. Cruise would've been allowed to play the bear in our script or any other role of his choosing. He was running hot. Since Ford passed, our next stop was Dustin Hoffman because his agent said he had read the script and was interested. A bird in the hand. Dustin Hoffman wasn't tearing up the box office as he once did, but he was still a star. Fox encouraged the flirtation.

This is always a tenuous time in the packaging of a movie. This is how it works: Even if the studio gets excited, even giddy, by the new script (as they claimed to be with *Bookworm*), the studio never calls the producer and says, 'We love this, we love you, here's the money, let's fire this baby up.' They always have several scripts in the pipeline that they fancy from different directors and/or producers. As optimistic and encouraging as they appear, they are simply not going to make all of them. The executives' collective enthusiasm for the material can bounce around like a baby's temperature. If Harrison Ford passes, their enthusiasm dips. If they think he passed but probably didn't personally read the damn thing, the dip begins to rise. If several actors or directors pass, their enthusiasm goes on life support. If you get a nibble as we'd gotten from Dustin, spirits lift. If and when he passes, confidence wanes, and eventually, as the rejections add up, finger-pointing inevitably follows: 'Who the fuck on my staff liked this piece of shit script anyhow?' 'Can you believe even Richard Gere couldn't make heads or tails of it?'

When this starts to happen, your best hope is that you have another script to work on because their intention to package this one will soon be transferred to fresher material. Knowing you're going to get some noes, you have to strategize not to get too many before the flame burns out. Just as on the TV game show *Let's Make a Deal*, newcomers to this game are continually led to door #1, #2, or #3 certain that the money is just on the other side, only to be tossed out at high speed in the middle of rush-hour traffic, screaming, 'But . . . but . . . but you said . . .' And your executive friend won't be flying out the door with you saying, 'I don't care what anyone thinks, I love this turkey and we're going to make it no matter where we have to go.' In fact, the word *we* is no longer used in conversation once you're off the lot.

From the agent's point of view, the terrain is just as tenuous. Some subtle issues are involved. If a client at the top of his power is deluged by offers, the agent won't give him or her the script without a firm offer from the studio. Except for rare instances the studio gulps and gives firm offers to very few. Today that may include Jim Carrey, Tom Cruise, and Julia Roberts. The list gets redefined yearly depending on recent successes or failures.

It can turn into an Abbott and Costello sketch:

'Could you please give my script to Harrison Ford?'

'Do you have a firm offer from Fox?'

'Well, not exactly, but they said they'd make the movie.'

'Harrison does not read without a firm pay or play offer.'

'But he might love it, really love it, and think his destiny lies in making this movie.'

'Pay to play.'

'But if he doesn't read it, he'll never know what he might miss.'

'Fifteen million against fifteen percent of the gross.'

'Okay, I'll talk to Bill.'

'By the way, Alan Alda is looking for something good, I can give it to him to read.'

'Gee, thanks, let me talk to Mechanic.'

Dustin Hoffman, with all of his past greatness, was now, as they say, *reading*. This euphemism means that he is willing to look at scripts without a firm offer, and if he is interested, he is willing to meet with the producer and the director. This is particularly good news for the studio, especially if the actor loves the script and the studio has yet to commit. The leverage builds logarithmically in their favor. If the executives at Fox agree to make the movie, they may be able to reduce the actor's price because they already know that he loves the script. Actors are like everyone else: When they want something they might not get, they often want it more. If Mechanic et al. decide not to make the movie, even if the actor is begging, they lose nothing and can make some apology for the inconvenience. The agent then gets the horror call: 'What kind of dickhead agent would send me a script that the studio won't make even if I liked it.' 'But . . . but, Dusty . . . but . . .' That's why agents are very, very careful how they distribute the material to their top clients. Since the studio heads don't know exactly what the total cost of the film is going to be, they are equally reluctant to expose themselves. It's the catch-22 of packaging, with the producer hopelessly in the middle, staring wide-eyed into space, having as much control over the situation as a busboy at Spago's.

Back in Dustin's office, another two hours had passed. We were in the middle of a lox-and-bagel lunch, and we had still not discussed the Mamet script. It's not that Dustin was avoiding it, he just seemed to have a lot of tangential interests. We talked about sports, current events, diet, religion. He even gave Lee and me some literature on a new rabbi who had captured his imagination. Occasionally, he would glance at my ankles.

Being the restless type, I was hoping to make a frontal assault. I kept looking at him, thinking, 'Fuck me. We're gonna die here. Are you gonna make this sucker or not?' But producers are not known for raw courage. All that I could muster was an occasional 'That is *so* interesting.' 'Really.' 'Gosh, I feel the same way, don't you, Lee?' Self-loathing was starting to creep in, and I decided to leave the meeting, hoping that in my absence they would begin to address the script. As I politely rose and told them I had had no idea this was going to be such a time-consuming first discussion, blah blah blah, I suggested that perhaps they could carry on without me. I glanced at Lee, with a stunned, wide-eyed signal: 'Try and wrap him up, please.' Lee looked at me as if to say, 'I'm from New Zealand, don't leave me here alone.' Clearly, we both had the sinking feeling that this exercise was sliding into the toilet.

When I was in the elevator, it occurred to me that Dustin had made one reference to the script about an hour earlier. He had said *Bookworm* reminded him of *Straw Dogs*. Since that Peckinpah movie was one of my favorites and since Dustin was so fine in it, I took this to be a good thing. Wrong. He'd done this part already! Of course! Bookish guy with a pretty, seductive wife having to rise to the occasion when the going got brutal. Dustin's a rich man. Why would he ever do the same part again? Perhaps Lee didn't know it yet, but it was time to look for someone else. Let's go back to the list. We could spend the next six months having nice chats with Dustin, but when the time came to put the chips on the table, I was sure he wasn't going to be there, and I was more sure I would have even less hair on my ankles.

FOUR

ONE PLUS ONE EQUALS THREE

lec Baldwin might be in. His agent said that Alec had read the script and wanted to talk about the role of the duplicitous fashion photographer, Bob Green. Lee and I greeted the news with measured enthusiasm. I knew that even if Alec was ideal casting, this news was never going to make the walls of the Fox administration building shake with delight. His past success was spotty, and there were rumors that he was difficult. At best, Alec would be considered a solid 'element' to the overall package, but not enough of a reason, I thought, for Fox to pull the trigger. It was the best nibble so far. We had to pursue it.

We agreed to meet with Alec for lunch at some trendy bistro off of La Cienega. Lee and I got there early to strategize, because these first encounters are always tricky. You don't know if the actor is flirting with the role or if he is actually hooked. But that first lunch does give you some indication as to how the dynamics are going to work if the movie actually gets put together. Is it going to be an easy ride, or are you going to be sliding down a gravel driveway together naked? When Alec arrived at the table, he was dressed in a suit and tie, looking as if he were running for a Long Island congressional seat. I got things started. Unable to camouflage my desperation to get a big-name actor to commit, I began with the predictable propitiating smiles and nods. 'Gosh you were brilliant in blah blah blah' and

'How about that speech in *Glengarry*, oh, man, it was an aria . . . wasn't it, Lee?' I couldn't control myself. To his credit, Alec responded to the horseshit flattery by saying he was a fan of David Mamet's writing and would be eager to take on this role. No caveats. Simple as that. He said he would have to complete the movie *Ghosts of Mississippi*, take a couple of months off to diet and to get into tip-top shape, and then he would be ready to go, assuming the studio was willing to write the check.

Unfortunately, this all happened in the first five minutes. We hadn't even ordered yet and I was ready to call for the check. It's an old maxim in Hollywood: Take yes for an answer and quickly leave the room. The rest of the lunch attenuated into awkward sound bites like 'God, this is really going to be great.' 'We're so damn excited.' 'Did I already tell you how much I love your work? . . . Of course I did.'

The only wrinkle for me – and at the time I did not give it much importance – was that Alec kept avoiding eye contact with Tama-hori, who was, after all, the director. Even though we were reduced to banal hiccups, it seemed at times as if Alec was pretending that Lee was at another table. I thought later that perhaps Alec had a genetic disdain for anyone who could exert power over his perfor-mance, so he did not want to cozy up to Lee too soon. Nonetheless, something in the air was casting a small shadow, but I ignored it. My job was to get the fucking movie made. If there were going to be difficulties, we would deal with them down the road. For now, we had a good actor anxious to do the part. After several weeks of rejections, Lee and I felt we might be edging ever closer to a start date.

The next day, I was seated in Bill Mechanic's office next to a large bowl of soft sugar candies, waiting for him to get off the phone. I would start each meeting swearing to Bill that I would not touch the candy. It was the kind of stuff you'd be embarrassed to hand out on

Halloween. But the anxiety of rarely getting what I wanted out of these meetings inevitably forced me into the candy bowl within minutes of our discussions.

'Good news. Alec Baldwin wants to play the photographer,' I opened confidently.

'I heard,' Bill said, not matching my enthusiasm.

'He's a wonderful actor.'

'He's expensive.'

'He has lots of energy.'

'I hear he hates producers.'

'Who doesn't these days?'

'He doesn't sell tickets.'

'What about *Hunt for Red October*?'

'That was a lifetime ago.'

'But it was huge.'

'What kinda guy walks away from the sequel after such a big hit and lets Harrison Ford take his place?'

I reached in the bowl for a green one.

'Bill, what about *Malice*?'

'Have you seen the numbers on *Malice*?'

'Not the foreign numbers.'

'Well, even *Malice* was a long time ago.'

'Lee and I think he's perfect for the part.'

'I hear he's trouble.'

'Beating up a photographer doesn't make you trouble. Anyway, it was in self-defense.'

'He can't carry a movie.'

'Bill, who can carry a movie?'

'Tom Cruise.'

'What are you saying?'

'I'm saying if you can find a star for the other part, then maybe we can match him up with Alec.'

'I'm always one star short.'

'You are one star short.'

In the delicate mechanism of Hollywood meetings, this was a positive exchange. Bill was basically saying that he really liked the material, that in fact he was seriously inclined to make the movie, but that he needed as much ammo as possible. His job was to protect the downside, to second-guess the options, and he did it in an amiable way. I knew he wanted more than a *good* movie, he wanted and needed a hit. Who can blame him. I needed a hit as well.

'Bill, why don't we make a deal with Alec now and make it subject to finding the other guy?'

'We can explore it, but I would also have to make the offer subject to a budget.'

'Well, then Fox wouldn't be bound at all.'

'That's right.' Bill smiled.

'Gee.'

'Hey, the other part's the real star of the movie anyway.'

'We think Alec's kind of a star.'

'Good, let's find another bigger star.'

'Sure, let's find a bigger star,' I said, reaching into the candy bowl for the last time.

I took a huge handful for the road.

After the mandate from Mechanic, I decided to talk to Robert De Niro. The part of Charles Morse, the aging, shy, erudite, bookish rich man, was not a role you would immediately feel was smart casting for De Niro – unless of course, he thought he could do it. If he said he was intent on playing the part of a seven-year-old ballerina in a Disney musical, I would have to take it seriously. Ever since *The Untouchables*, Bob and I have remained close friends. It's not just that his shining performance saved my ass, got us on the cover of *Newsweek*, and made me and everyone else connected to the movie look like we knew what we were doing, but we really found a way to connect. It was an unusual dynamic. I would say things like 'Gosh, Bob, you sure make a lot of money acting in those movies,' and he would answer, 'Lemme get back to you.' I would say, 'What do you think of that director or that writer or that actor,' and he would say, 'Lemme get back to you.' I would say, 'I think you should consider this script. It would be great for you, you should really do it,' and he would say, 'What is it you do, again?' You get the gist of it. But just because you've had a long-term relationship with Bob doesn't necessarily mean that you can get him to act in your movie. It does mean, however, that you might be able to get him to read something without a firm offer from the studio. When the script was first completed, I wanted to send it to him, but he was so booked up with other pictures that the timing was bad. It would have been too easy for him to say no. By the time Lee and I had slogged through the predictable turndowns, the timing had improved. I forged ahead. I gave Bob *Bookworm* and awaited his response.

My phone rang.

'Hey.'

'Hey.'

'What'd ya think?'

'I like it.'

'How much?'

'I like it.'

'How about Alec Baldwin for the photographer?'

'I like him.'

'Great. Let's do it.'

'I like it, it's got some good things in it.'

'Great, let's go.'

'I think we need a reading.'

'But you just read it.'

'I think we should have a *reading*.'

'Let me read it to you over the phone.'

'We should have a *reading*.'

This categorically means the deal is far from closed. When he'd agreed to do *The Untouchables*, he did not ask for a reading. This response of his was a bit better than being on life support, but way too soon to open the Veuve Clicquot.

'Fine, let's have a reading.'

'You set it up. It would be nice if Alec was there.'

'I hate readings.'

'Set up a reading.'

'Fine.'

For those of you unfamiliar with a *reading*, this is different from the notion that an actor is reading without an offer. This sort of reading is when several actors sit around a table and read the script out loud. Someone is usually chosen to read the narrative and the descriptive sections.

For example:

EXT. SAPLINGS – DAY

The bear crashes through and follows Morse at a frightening speed. Just as the bear is about to bring him down, Morse reaches the other side of the clearing and scrambles through a small gap between a tangle of heavy logs. The bear is unable to follow through the gap and cannot get at Morse, who backs up terrified.

The bear ROARS.

Sometimes the narrator will actually attempt a roar, but most likely he will just say 'roar.' No matter how it sounds, ten directors would render this scene ten different ways. The remaining dialogue in the script is read by other actors with varying degrees of commitment. If you are an actor or a director who is grappling with committing to the material, the reading is supposed to provide some special insight, some connection, that sitting at home, quietly perusing the script, would not give. It's a high-stakes game with sizable decisions riding on its outcome. When readings go badly, you not only lose those actors you were trying to attract, you might lose those actors who were already committed. In this case, if De Niro decides *Bookworm* would not be for him, would that send Baldwin running away as well, shrieking, 'Thank the Lord! It's only a scratch. I'm out of here.'? A project can quickly skid off the road without much chance of recovery. For me, readings are always an iffy affair. Let's face it, we watch movies, we don't listen to them.

The creamy-colored conference room at the Peninsula Hotel had a 'crafts service' table set up in the corner with the usual: coffee, rolls, lox and bagels, soft drinks, bottled water, fruit, etc. A copy of the script was positioned in front of each chair. David Mamet, who lived in Boston, would not be attending. Knowing David, if Boston were a suburb of Beverly Hills and I offered to 'send the limo,' he would still call in sick. His reaction would be 'Just tell 'em to say the fuckin' words.' This probably was not the best sentiment to have in the room.

Lee and I, as hosts, were the first to arrive, soon followed by a couple of actors who had been asked to read the smaller parts. The tacit understanding at these events is that it is not an audition, that readers should not expect to get a part, and that they aren't expected to 'perform.' Inevitably, however, these actors are the most spirited in the room. With the presence of De Niro and a real live director listening, why shouldn't they audition? It's in their DNA.

Minutes before Alec showed up, Bryan Lourd, one of De Niro's agents from CAA, arrived dressed in the new neo-pallbearer fashion (narrow black suit, black tie, black shoes). It was Saturday afternoon and I couldn't help but feel that as smooth as Bryan was, a cheerier look would have been more comforting. When Alec finally entered, his demeanor was slightly more edgy than it had been at the restaurant. This time, he wasn't making eye contact with Lee or with me. I tried to dismiss it, assuming that the anticipation of reading with De Niro would make any actor anxious. Frankly, all of his furtive angst and sweaty energy made him perfect for the part of Green. He introduced himself around the room, took a seat at the table, and waited.

Another fifteen minutes passed and Bob was late. Lee and I looked at each other as if we were waiting for Elvis. I wondered how much Bryan Lourd's enthusiasm would influence De Niro's decision. Bryan was sitting away from the table, intentionally out of the line of fire, looking like a calming influence at a funeral. My optimism was waning. Bob finally showed up, followed by a couple of assistants, and Alec's mood noticeably improved. But despite all of the expected titillation that came with the 'Elvis' arrival, when Bob passed through the door, quiet and unassuming, his demeanor was as nondescript as a family accountant's. I knew that he was aware of his impact, but there was no evidence that he wanted any part of it. Wearing fatherly glasses and clothes that would go unnoticed in the local mall – if we weren't sure it was him, De Niro would have been asked to leave the room.

The greetings went rapidly around the table. It was evident that Bob actually wanted to 'hear' the script. No other agenda. We began the reading with the narrator announcing, 'Fade-in.'

Mamet's dialogue is very different from standard Hollywood fare. Not every actor can find a way into it to make it sound real and unforced. For example, forty pages into this script, a plane crash leaves Green (Baldwin) and Morse (De Niro) lost in the wilds of Alaska trying to keep from being eaten by a determined bear. Morse and Green banter about Morse's wife, the fashion model to be photographed by Green. She was left at base camp.

GREEN
Hey, is it my diseased imagination,
or did you say the words, 'How are you
trying to kill me?'

(pause) Morse nods.

GREEN (cont'd)
And what did that mean . . . ?
Why would I want to kill you, Charles?
Why would I want to do that?

MORSE
For my wife.

GREEN
For *Mickey*? (pause)
Well, *that's* a bizarre way to meet girls . . .
I want to *kill* you to get next to your
wife?

MORSE
. . . I've seen you with her.

GREEN
No offense, Charles, I can get my
own girl. F'you perhaps noticed that
in the time we've known each other?
N'pee ess, you're kind of a powerful
guy. Why would someone want to
antagonize you?
(pause)

I'm talking to you. Why?
    MORSE
To get the money.

    GREEN
Ooooh. The money . . . Now it's
the broad, now it's the boodle . . .
nothing is safe.
   (pause)
That's what I'm saying . . . Rich man.
All anybody wants, *take* something from
you. And they want it bad enough to
kill you.
   (pause)
You know what . . . the rich *are* different.

Alec wasn't reading this stuff, he was performing it with gusto. 'Now it's the broad, now it's the boodle?' He took to Mamet's language and cadences like a dog to hamburger meat. For those of you who have seen his cameo in *Glengarry Glen Ross*, he fills Mamet's characters with extraordinary life. I glanced over at Lee, thinking, 'Hey, this is gonna work, Alec's gonna knock the shit out of this part. Let's get out there and make this baby.'

Bob, on the other hand, was delivering his reading of Morse in an expressionless monotone. Very simple. One word following another, making no attempt to *do* anything. For the first ten minutes, I wondered if this was some charade, a bad breakfast, or perhaps some way of letting me down gently: 'Oh, well, I tried.' That sort of thing. As the reading went on, Bob continued with the same flat delivery. Everyone else in the room became more animated just to make up for it. Now when the bear roared, the narrator really roared. Whatever Bob was intending to put up on the screen, I knew it couldn't be this. Weeks later, when we were alone, I brought up the subject.

'What were you doing in the reading?'

'As readings go, I thought it was a good one.'

'Easy for you, you weren't doing anything.'

'What do you mean?'

'One word after the other, no emotion.'

'It was very helpful.'

'You were Mr. Robotman in there, how can you tell if it's working?'

'I can tell.'

'Why not rev up the engine a little bit?'

'That wouldn't be right.'

'Why?'

'Because if I haven't yet *made a decision* as to what I want to do, I don't want to *do* anything. For me, it's better to do nothing than to make false or careless choices.'

'All right then, s'all I wanted to know.'

As usual, Bob was ahead of the curve. As the reading wound down to the climactic moment of killing the bear, the narrator continued:

The bear turns on Morse. Green staggers to his feet and winces in pain as he sees Morse and the bear in mortal combat.

MORSE (De Niro)
Kill me! You killed my friend . . .
It doesn't matter anymore . . .
Kill me!!

The bear attacks. Morse holds his ground. The bear surges towards him. At the last moment, Morse drops the butt of the

spear down against the boulder and angles the spear up into
the bear as it charges.

I glanced over at Bob, noticing what I believed to be a slight flicker of
interest. Maybe he was warming to this thing. I now realize I was
grasping at straws. His twitch could have been anything. It was so
slight it could have been gas.

The bear closes over Morse and lunges. The spear tears
through the bear's back as the bear ROARS and drops on top of
Morse. As Green watches, the bear dies.

For a moment nothing moved.

Except for Bob. I definitely noticed a wince and a forward body motion.
He was thinking about it. The reading soon ended, and everyone went
his separate way. It was not the time or the place to ask the unaskable:
'Are you going to agree to do this fucking script or what?' Bryan Lourd
walked out nodding with an inscrutable expression. He whispered to
me, 'I'll call you later.' Alec seemed happy. He knew that he was going
to cream this part if we ever did get the movie off the ground. And Lee
and I were cautiously pleased. If we had discovered nothing else, we
had at least confirmed that this was going to be a compelling story. We
just had to cast Morse and get the money.

I met Bob later for a drink. I knew as soon as I saw him walk in
that he was not going to do the part. You learn to read the signals. It's
not what he does, it's what he doesn't do. And I also knew that he
probably wouldn't share his exact feelings as to why.

'Don't say anything, I can tell it's over.'

'What?'

'You're not gonna commit.'

'I like it.'

'There's a problem.'

'The bear worries me.'

'The bear?!'

'The bear.'

'Y'sure it's not Alec or Lee?'

'For now, it's the bear.'

'What part of the bear?'

'You know, fighting with a fake bear. Might not work.'

'We're gonna use a real bear some of the time.'

'A real bear is interesting.'

'Well, then we're gonna use a real bear a lot.'

A beat.

'The bear . . . the bear still concerns me.'

There was no sense in belaboring this. Bob was not going to do the movie.

Well, actually, a week later, I decided to take one more shot. I was able to get a rough cut of *Mulholland Falls*, the picture that Lee Tamahori had just finished for Dick and Lilly Zanuck, and I set up a private screening in Santa Monica for Bob's and my eyes only. I told Bob that I understood trying to say, 'Are you looking at me . . . are YOU looking at ME?' to a mechanical bear (or even a real bear) might be a tall order, but perhaps after seeing Lee's movie he might have a change of heart. Bob responded, 'Maybe we can have the bear fuck the photographer, that might be interesting.'

When the lights slowly came up, he reached for his cell phone and started dialing. I did not perceive this as good news. When we got outside, I pressed him for his thoughts.

'Whataya think?'

'The hats.'

'The hats!'

'All the actors kept their hats on throughout the movie.'

'I noticed that.'

'It's not right.'

'Can't we put the hats aside?'

'I don't know.'

He made another call from his cell phone. This was clearly going nowhere.

'What were you wearing at the reading?' Jerry asked. We were waiting for our cars outside the Ivy.

'What difference does it make?'

'Well, I had to sit through a description of the CAA couture look.'

'It's just not relevant.'

'I think it is.'

'Trust me, it's not.'

'Lemme guess. Black leather sport coat, tattered T-shirt, faded Levi's, and Prada loafers without socks.'

'This is stupid.'

'Dressing like a fat Don Johnson is stupid.'

'Frankly, Jerry, what I was wearing is not the point.'

'I'm right, aren't I?'

'No.'

'I think so.'

'No . . . I would never wear Prada loafers.'

A black-on-black BMW came up from the underground garage; three people simultaneously reached for the driver's door before they realized it wasn't their car.

'It's not that this story of yours about *readings* is dull,' Jerry continued. 'But if you weren't paying for lunch, I would have been facedown in my crab cakes.'

'It's background.'

'But where's the suspense? We know *Sir* Anthony Hopkins ended up with the job.'

'I thought you wanted me to go slow.'

'Hell, next time let me smell some blood.'

'I aim to please.'

Rick Nicita, Anthony Hopkins's agent, called to say his client wanted the part of Charles Morse. This was a particularly good call because there were no strings attached, no qualifications. Hopkins signed off on the script, loved the idea of doing it with Alec Baldwin, had seen Tamahori's first movie, thought it was excellent, and was ready to approve him. Check! All that was left, once I finessed the predictably annoying naysayings of Tom Rothman, was Bill Mechanic's and Peter Chernin's endorsements.

It had become evident over the last few months that Chernin was increasingly taking himself out of the line of fire. Where he used to engage directly in the major green-light decisions, now Mechanic was the only one in the room. Chernin was exhibiting expert Teflon instincts. He had no choice. *Titanic* was in the middle of production and the costs were staggering out of control. While I was trying to get this small movie launched, Fox was completely absorbed and distracted by James Cameron. With astonishing costs and an un-quenchable appetite, Cameron was making it crystal clear that he was not going to quit until the batteries ran out. Chernin knew he had to cushion the fall. He bravely decided to let Bill jump in front of the bus and try to slow it down.

James Cameron, after making *Aliens* and *True Lies* for Fox, was a company star long before either Mechanic or Chernin were ever considered for their jobs. This made dealing with him an extra-ordinary task. Who would want to be the guinea pig to tell this guy to stop spending money? Rumor has it that when Bill was sent to Rosarito Beach, Mexico, to try to put a tourniquet on the wound, Cameron demanded that Bill not only leave the set but also leave the country and that he would not continue filming until Mechanic was gone. If you're the head of a studio, this is like getting a prostate exam courtside at a Laker game during halftime. 'We're doing spectacle,' Cameron said. 'And spectacle costs money.' Bill handled all of this madness with a solid equanimity. He wanted this job and he was willing to put up with an awful lot of abuse to hold on to it.

How corporately savvy for Chernin to be in a position to say to Rupert that Mechanic was the guy to be on top of this mess. What a luxury. When the costs rocketed past $100 million, he could say, 'Rupert, I told that son of a bitch that the movie was going to get too expensive, and he better get that director to toe the line.' When the movie crossed the $150-million mark, he could say, 'Don't worry, Rupert, three strikes and Mechanic's out of here.' And when the explosion hit $200 million, he could say, 'You know, Rupert, it's so damn hard to find good help these days.' With all of the chaos that was swirling at Fox, the myriad decisions that had to be made on other movies seemed less monumental.

It was a good time to get something done.

Putting Tony Hopkins and Alec Baldwin together for the first time was perfect casting artistically. Both were extraordinary actors. Both were perfectly suited for their respective roles. Hopkins playing a bookish, gentle rich man lost in the wilderness having to survive with Baldwin, playing a younger, slicker, duplicitous photographer who was planning to kill him and take his wife and his money, was an exciting combination. The only hitch (and I knew that it would soon surface) is the perception that Anthony Hopkins doesn't really 'sell tickets,' another Hollywood euphemism for 'He ain't no Tom Hanks.' Who is?

I came up with an ingenious way to sell this stew. Since neither actor can 'carry' a movie by himself, according to studio executives who were pulling up their past grosses over the last few years, why not view this combination of actors as logarithmically larger than the whole? The idea being that Hopkins plus Baldwin is much bigger than either of them alone. And that, maybe, just maybe, the two together would equal one big, fat movie star. Think about it. Would you trade one Keanu Reeves for Edward Norton with Richard Gere? Maybe. It was clear from the start that if we'd attracted a Tom Cruise, we could have cast the rest of the movie with actors who 'don't sell tickets.' But that didn't happen.

'Bill, I've got a theory.'

'Oh, here it comes.'

'One plus one equals three.'

'I don't get it.'

'*One plus one equals three*.'

'You need something to clear your head.'

'Stay with me.'

'I'm not leaving.'

'Don't ya think one Hopkins and one Baldwin together for the first time on the screen equals one Harrison Ford?'

'No. Absolutely not.'

'Bill, together these guys are gonna sell tickets. I feel the sizzle.'

'They might . . . but I'm *certain* Harrison Ford *will*.'

'Go with me . . . the sum of these guys is greater than the parts.'

'I learned to add differently from you.'

'Trust me on this.'

'I don't need to 'cause we're going to make the movie anyway.'

'I don't care if . . . come again.'

'If we can make their deals and you can make the movie for under thirty million dollars, we'll green-light it.'

'I'll take yes for an answer.'

Obviously, my little theory wasn't the catalyst that had pushed Bill into a start date. Over the last several weeks he had been pushing Lee and me to deliver the best possible package without putting Fox at risk. He knew after our exhaustive search that Hopkins and Baldwin was as far as we were going to get. And it wasn't too shabby. Making it at the thirty-million number would be right at the risk line for this kind of picture. Between video, DVD, foreign, and cable, it would only have to perform modestly in the United States for Fox to get their investment back. Even though it might have lacked the sexiness of a Brad Pitt movie or the grandness of a *Titanic*, it was still a good piece of business. Fox's huge distribution system had to be fed, and not all pictures are going to feel like slam dunks. With this cast, Bill could commiserate with Chernin, and neither would be called out for embarrassing themselves.

As I left Bill's office, we shook hands.

'By the way,' he said. 'One plus one equals two.'

'If you say so, it's so.'

FIVE

AFTER SHAVE

Canmore, a picturesque small town nestled in the Rockies about sixty miles west of the Calgary airport, was chosen as the production headquarters for *Bookworm*. With towering mountains and expansive forests, it was an ideal location to film an outdoor adventure picture. We decided to build a lodge on a nearby lake, and the rest of the locations would primarily be found in the surrounding wilds. The actual shooting of the movie, compressed to fifty-five days, went along rather uneventfully. There were, of course, the occasional complications from using an eighteen-hundred pound real bear. But, all in all, our man-eating 'Bart the Bear' was a total pro. He could give us several different looks, growl on command, and even do comedy if it was required. Lee kept referring to him as John Wayne. The anamatronic bear, which we spent hundreds of thousands of dollars to construct, turned out to be less effective. Next to a real bear who can 'act,' a robot bear becomes extremely artificial. As filming progressed, the fake bear spent more and more time in the prop truck. He was our insurance policy, our pinch hitter.

Shortly after the movie was released, Bart often received as much or more attention than the rest of the cast. Norm MacDonald, on *Saturday Night Live*, said, while pointing to a large picture of Tony Hopkins and Alec Baldwin bravely trying to ward off the bear, 'Bart the Bear delivered an outstanding performance and was paid in raw meat, bear whores, and cocaine.'

A brief scare did occur during filming. Hopkins, who was taking painkillers for a severe pinched nerve in his neck, went down with hypothermia after spending several hours in freezing water enacting the plane crash. Apparently, the painkillers were so deadening that he couldn't feel the harsh, icy conditions. While in the hospital for the hypothermia, the pain from his neck without painkillers became so acute that an immediate operation was necessary. This caused a shutdown of production for several days. As you might imagine, with all of the genuine concerns for our star, the real relief for the studio execs came when they were assured that the entire incident was covered by insurance. The calls to Tony were 'Get well soon, big guy,' and the calls to us were 'What's our deductible, what's our deductible?!' The English-knighted Hopkins, who had yet to become an American citizen, showed his valor by maintaining a 'stiff upper lip' and soldiering on with a quiet smile.

One wrinkle, however, had a far-reaching and dampening effect on the morale of the whole shoot. The problem began ten days before principal photography – nothing so severe as careening off the side of a cliff at high speed, but still, for Lee and me, what was initially anticipated to be an idyllic summer-camp romp for grown-ups turned into a psychobabble set filled with hidden tensions.

Lee decided it would be a good idea to take one more look at the script. He called for a reading the following morning in the large conference facility that had been built for the 1988 Winter Olympics. A final script run-through would provide that last overview for the director to examine the material as a whole. There is an old showbiz maxim once shooting starts: From then on, making a movie is like eating an elephant with a teaspoon – one nibble at a time. One last look at the script can be a good idea. Since everyone in the room already had his or her respective job, these readings were usually relaxed and fun.

Tamahori, Elle Macpherson, who had landed the cameo of Hopkins's trophy wife, Harold Perrineau, the photographer's assistant, L. Q. Jones, the lodge owner, Don Macalpine, the cinematographer, the script girl, and me were seated around the conference table when Alec and Tony entered the room. For those working behind the scenes, seeing two stars together for the first time can be heady stuff. After the first week of photography the exhilaration quickly turns to work and becomes old hat, but in those first few days, we are reduced to hopeless fans. And in an odd way, you can sense that the performers feel the same sense of awe for each other.

I had just arrived from New York and I hadn't seen Alec since that odd reading at the Peninsula Hotel in Beverly Hills several months before. Surprisingly, Alec was wearing a full beard. Not just your average beard; this beard had run amok. It looked as if he had entered a Grizzly Adams look-alike contest. I assumed he probably wanted to see what he was going to look like when he was stranded out in the wilds for several weeks. Like any diligent actor, particularly someone as intense as Alec, he was simply exploring the character. It had an interesting impact. Twenty pounds heavier than he had been at our lunch, and with the flowing gray beard, he had completely stripped himself of his leading-man looks. The effect made him look older than Hopkins. No longer the predatory good-looking lothario who was the character at the onset of the film, Alec looked like the beaten man who was to be bested by a bookworm out in the wilds. I thought, what a clever and effective way to explore the character by experiencing the end first.

As they started going through the script, Alec and Tony took the material to new heights. Even though Morse/Hopkins knows that Green/Baldwin has tried to kill him and steal his wife and money, toward the end of the sceenplay Morse still attempts to save the gravely wounded Green. The conference room was completely still:

MORSE
Don't die on me. Bob.

GREEN
. . . I . . . I don't feel, uh, uh, a hundred percent.

MORSE
Why don't you save your strength?

GREEN
What's the point of it, you see?
I'm dying.

MORSE
Hold on, Bob. Hold on. I'll make a fire . . .

GREEN
. . . Now I'm your pet project . . . Is that it Charles? I'm your hobby farm.

MORSE
That's right, Bob.

GREEN
No. I know what it is . . . you never had a buddy. That's the thing, isn't it . . . ?

MORSE
. . . If you say so.

GREEN

Hey, why would you want to save a piece of shit like me?

MORSE

. . . Say it's a challenge.

When all is lost and it's clear that Green is not going to make it:

MORSE

Don't die . . . Bob.

GREEN

(looking back with a smile)

Charles, don't tell me what to do.

Everyone applauded. Listening to these actors read Mamet's stuff was like watching butter melt. We briefly talked about some minor script changes to take up with Mamet, and the reading was adjourned.

As Lee and I walked to our cars, we reviewed the situation:

'They're gonna be great, huh?' I said.

'Truly.'

'What's with the beard thing?'

'Don't know.'

'Did you tell him to shave?'

'No.'

'Lee, tell'm he can wear a beard at the end of the movie.'

'I'm going to bring it up, but I haven't done it yet.'

'If he doesn't shave, Fox will go nuts.'

'We have a week. I'm sure he plans on shaving.'

'I thought so when he walked in, y'know, sort of exploring the character blah blah, but after seeing him read, I sensed this is going to be his look.'

'We got time.'

'Lee, let me explain the Fox situation. They didn't really want to hire this guy in the first place. Rothman kept wailing that he's overpriced and Bill agreed. The guy cost five million dollars, for God's sake.'

'Hey, that's your department.'

'For that kind of money, they thought they'd at least bought a younger leading man to balance out Hopkins. If Mechanic thought Alec was going to enter this fight overweight, bearded, and old, his price would have been two free dinners at Spago and ten percent of the net.'

'I'll tell Alec tomorrow he's got to shave.'

'I got a bad feeling.'

'He's probably just getting into character.'

'Here's hopin', 'cause Fox's demographics for this movie will be limited to retirement villages in Boca Raton.'

'I gotta go check on the mechanical bear.'

'I can see the ad line now: "See Gabby Hayes run."'

'Don't worry, he'll shave.'

'I hope so.'

It was a beautiful day in the Rockies. I decided to drive out to the lake to see how the construction of the lodge was progressing. I veered off Main Street, entered the highway next to Bow Valley Trail, and drove directly into the mountains. As I turned on Canmore's oldies rock station, I fully expected Creedence's 'Bad Moon Rising' to come blasting through the speakers, confirming my paranoia. Since Alec's relations with Lee and me were limited to occasional random, furtive glances, having to ask Alec, 'That beard's quite a look, what are *we* going to do about that?' was, at the very least, unpleasant. I knew actors. My imagination for misery started to take on a life of its own. 'If the son of a bitch doesn't shave, it's going to get ugly, it's going to be a shit storm' became the predominant head theme. I had to get a grip. Alec would surely realize that Green was supposed to go from slick New York fashion photographer to mountain man. Why was I obsessing about this? After all, we had more than a week before we burned some film, and there was no hard evidence that Alec was going to hold on to the Long Island Santa Claus look. At least not once he thought it through. This was much ado about nothing.

As I got closer to the lodge, the clean air and the exhilaration of the scenery overtook any darker thoughts. In fact, for a brief moment, I was consumed by the producer's ultimate movie perk. To be in such a truly beautiful spot, watch a movie get made, and get paid for it was a sinful pleasure to be privately enjoyed. Don't get me wrong, being able to occasionally tell an agent or an executive, 'I'm sorry, I'm going to have to pass, go fuck yourself,' was also a guilty pleasure that ranks high on the Hollywood ladder. But, the serenity of being in the middle of the majestic Rockies, on someone else's dime, was the brass ring.

'Motherfucker. MOTHERFUCKER!'

'But, Alec, if you—'

'MOTHERFUCKING movie PRODUCER. I knew this was coming, the bullshit Hollywood mentality telling ME ... MOTHERFUCKER!'

Alec calmly placed his leather jacket on an empty chair near the rear wall of the wardrobe trailer. The two girls who were fitting him were directly in the line of fire. They remained frozen. It had been three days and Lee was unable to pop the question, so I finally jumped in with my best version of 'When's the beard gonna go?' I looked over at Lee, who was seated next to me at the fitting table trying to absorb the magnitude of the explosion. It wasn't quite the response for which we had hoped.

'But . . . you get to grow the beard back once—'

'No-talent, MOTHERFUCKING . . . How predictable to see that good old Hollywood INTEGRITY at work.' He walked over to the wardrobe stand, feinted a kick, and then decided to let one go. The fitting girls fled from the trailer.

'Integrity! Producer, my ass!'

My first thought, of course, was to say, 'You asshole! I'm one of the guys who does the floors and windows so a schmuck like you can get your picture taken outside Mr. Chow's. SO BLOW ME!' But for lack of courage or just my genetic propensity to protect the bottom line, I tried to restrain myself.

'Alec, if you want to talk about integrity . . . let's talk about integrity. If YOU want to talk about INTEGRITY!' But, there I went. Up, up, and away. I couldn't help myself. I made the ultimate mistake. I began to take this personally. I lead with my chin. 'I'm willing to stack my last five pictures against your last five pictures. Let's go.'

He slowly walked toward us. He looked at me, avoided Lee, and smashed his first directly in the middle of the makeshift table. It started to buckle. 'Motherfucker,' he whispered. Then with impeccable timing he turned and left the trailer.

Lee and I peered at each other, our faces knotted into twisted grins. Dignity was an affectation.

'I don't think he expects to shave,' I said.

'You can say that,' Lee added.

I felt for Lee. Both of us knew that directing this guy, under these conditions, wasn't going to be easy. I also felt for Alec. He had something in mind when he grew that beard. Even if we felt it was wrong, he was committed to it. Having to make a change like that becomes personal.

I called Mechanic to make him aware of the situation. He was unequivocal. If Alec didn't cut the beard, we would shut down until he was replaced. Mechanic recommended Bill Pullman, who had just had a large part in *Independence Day*. Bill suggested that Pullman would probably love to work with Mamet material and with Hopkins and, more important, would probably do it for no money. I could tell that Mechanic was getting revved up about the thought of saving millions of dollars. Unfortunately, this choice wasn't going to work for Lee or for me. With all of the impending horror, Alec was still a talented actor and we wanted him. Hell, his performance in the wardrobe trailer alone proved that he was perfect for the part.

Bill recommended that I draw the line in the sand with Alec's agent, John Burnham from the William Morris office. We were running out of time. It was Thursday. Monday morning we were supposed to start shooting.

'You're kidding me.'

'No, John, I'm not kidding.'

I could hear it in his voice, a slight death rattle. John, who was an experienced agent, knew what it meant to be the messenger of this kind of news. He had no choice. Alec was a mercurial client, but Alec paid lots of commissions. For several seconds John remained silent. I sensed the mental machinery churning. He was mulling, 'Oh, I see . . . now I have to call my crazed client, a man who has the same affection for agents as Hitler had for Jews, and tell him to lop off his beard or he will be fired by the studio and sued for millions of dollars . . . piece a cake.' It was Burnham who had convinced Alec to do the movie in the first place.

'This can't be happening.'

'It's definitely happening.'

'Hey, let him wear his beard.'

'Oh, I'm afraid we're way past that.'

'Yesterday everything was fine, how did we get WAY PAST THAT in one day?'

'Mechanic thought Alec was overpriced anyway; he wouldn't mind if Alec went south. Save some money.'

'Have you told him about the shutting-down thing?'

'No, John, he left before we had a chance.'

'What about *lawsuit*? Did you mention the word *lawsuit*?'

'I didn't feel it was the right time.'

'You mean I have to tell him?'

'Yes.'

I could hear John's breathing getting heavier. He knew he had to put on the blindfold and get a cigarette. I didn't envy him.

'Hey, that's why you get the big bucks,' I said, trying to lighten up the call.

'I'll get back to you.'

Click.

'We got till Monday.'

Traditionally, the first day of shooting, getting that first shot *in the can*, was an exciting and tension-filled time. It was the signature that said, 'This baby is launched.' There would be no going back. After all of the nasty wrestling that it takes to get a movie set up, the first shot heralded that the movie was, for sure, going to get made. The studio usually sent you a basket of fruit or a leather folder. Past acrimony was replaced with sentiments of 'break a leg' or 'knock 'em dead.' Unfortunately, when Monday morning arrived, we were still uncertain if Alec was going to show up sans beard ready for work. Many calls were traded, but not even his lawyer knew where this was going. Were we to break out the champagne or shut the sucker down? By this time, the entire cast and crew were invested in the suspense.

As we were huddled by the frozen lake preparing to film the first setup, Alec finally arrived in a large SUV and quickly walked into his trailer. Lee and I only caught a glimpse, but he was clean-shaven. The crew was about to cheer but they knew better. Our feelings were mixed. We were pleased that we were going to get on with it but pained that with Alec so pissed off the next ten weeks could be difficult. I remember when he finished with hair and makeup and arrived on the set. I tried to stand off in the distance slightly hidden by one of the large fir trees. I didn't want my presence to come off as gloating. As the first shot between Hopkins, Alec, and Harold Perrineau was in final rehearsal by the camera, I couldn't help but notice that when Lee was talking, Alec would look only at Hopkins. Direct eye contact between Tamahori and Baldwin was nonexistent for the remainder of the shoot. As for my appearances on the set, I remained one hundred feet from Alec at all times, as if I had been served with a restraining order.

Once this impasse got reduced to what Hollywood classically calls 'a dick-waving incident,' the downward spiral of tensions became irreversible. I suppose there was no sense grousing about it; I should have found a way to avoid it. In the end, Alec's performance was applauded as truly excellent. John Burnham paid the price by losing his client. The oddest admission of all, however, is that, looking back, I am not convinced that Alec's performance or the ultimate box office fate of the movie would have been affected by the beard one way or the other.

Months later, I asked an actor friend of mine why Alec would have been so insistent on not shaving his beard. What sort of funky Stanislavsky decision would make him so committed? My friend said, without hesitation, 'Alec probably thought he was a little too heavy and he didn't like the way his chin looked.'

SIX

BOOKWORMED

'THE *Bookworm* is a terrible title. *Bookworm* is a terrific title,' Mamet was beseeching me on the phone, but apparently he wasn't getting my drift.

'Let me explain myself. Fox's marketing division doesn't like *The Bookworm, Bookworm, Green Bookworm, Any Sorta Bookworm*.'

'*Bookworm* is a good title.'

'They want to change it.'

'Isn't this a little late in the game?'

'It's very late in the game, we open in three months.'

'They're ridiculous.'

'They never let you down.'

'What's the next step?'

'They're making up lists.'

'What do we do?'

'We think of another name or they think of another name.'

'I like *Bookworm*.'

'I know. Unfortunately, it's not going to pass the shopping-center test.'

'I see.'

'Dave, I know it's hard to believe that, after all of this work, one's fate can be sealed by a group of pet-store owners in a suburb.'

'Ain't it so.'

Once a movie is completed, it gets turned over, so to speak, to the 'marketing' wizards whose job it is to sell the movie. These people try to figure out the best plan to convince tens of millions of people to leave their houses, park their cars, wait in line, pay their money, and sit through a movie on the opening weekend. If people collectively decide not to come out on that first Friday night, the movie sinks like a rock and ends up in video bins. Marketing seems like a heady, volatile job with much reponsibility. With all of the precarious success and failure of movies, you would think that the people who have these jobs would get hired and fired like fast-food cooks, but nothing could be further from the truth. If a movie fails miserably, they may execute the director, the writer, or the producer at sunrise (leaving them at the least on life support, hoping to get another chance), but as it turns out, the only one safer than a studio head is the head of marketing. It's never his fault.

How so? Without getting too tedious, marketing approaches most releases with what I refer to as the 'diminished expectations method.' After seeing the picture for the first time, the head of marketing (who in this case is Robert Harper) usually scratches his head, proclaims that this movie's going to be a tough one to sell, but that they'll do their level best to pull the rabbit out of the hat. This, of course, puts the filmmakers and the film executives on their heels because after all the work that has been done, if you can't sell the thing, the whole process becomes a hopeless exercise. It's as if the surgeon comes out in the middle of the operation, shaking his head saying, 'I'm gonna have to dig deep on this one, pull out all the stops, and then sew him back up. I don't know, but this might be a good time for prayer.' If the patient lives, the doctor is a hero. If the worst occurs, it was God's will, a patient who had no good reason to live. The doctor, always blameless, simply goes on to the next patient.

Bob Harper has been at Fox for over fifteen years. He took a brief time-out to try his hand at movie producing, but like his cohort Tom

Rothman smartly scurried back to the safe asylum of corporate security. At first glance you're struck by his calmness. Always casually dressed in the latest Banana Republic uniform, he conducts his meetings while occasionally taking practice putts on his carpet. Even though he was a minnow in the News Corp food chain, back in his secluded set of offices he was, to quote Tom Wolfe, 'master of his universe.' Except for the occasional blockbuster or a mega result from an preordained sequel, most of the movies that Harper devises campaigns for fail. This fact is ameliorated by the larger fact that most movies fail. Harper was accustomed to dying on Friday night only to be reborn on Monday morning ready to service the next Fox movie waiting to come out.

I noticed that Harper looked ten years younger than his age. Come to think of it, the marketeers at other studios also had that youthful glow of imperturbability. Harper was clearly onto something. His fountain of youth was knowing how to duck. If a movie worked, it was a goddamn great campaign. If a movie failed, well, you get the drill, the movie had an incurable cancer. He had properly warned all concerned that he had tried his best. If required, he was able to act as if he were truly saddened by the film's demise. He didn't get all misty-eyed, but he wanted the filmmakers to believe that this loss was his loss too. It was always a helluva performance.

After Harper saw an early rough cut of *Bookworm*, he told me that it was a very good movie (there's that *good* word cropping up again), but, of course, he had some grave concerns. I'm quite sure he gave the same response to Chernin, Mechanic, Rothman, et al. First, he said we were going to have to do something about *that* title, since his gut told him that it was going to turn people off. I asked whether the title should be tested, but Harper said testing titles was a waste of time. He didn't trust the results. 'You can test movies or trailers or even one sheets [movie posters] at random shopping malls,' he said, 'but not titles.' When he uttered the word *Bookworm*, his face would pucker as if he were trying to rid himself of the remnants of a fart. He said, in this case, 'I have to trust my insides.' Mechanic and Rothman shared his vision.

And, by the way, Harper wanted everyone to know that this was going to be a difficult movie to *sell*. The demographics were shit. Hadn't we realized that the favorable audience for Tony Hopkins and Alec Baldwin skewed over thirty? And surely, everyone knew that movies with lots of action skewed under thirty. No getting around it, action was our soup du jour. Just when we begin to care for the photographer's assistant, our bear viciously rips him to pieces and eats him. According to my calculations, if Harper's analyses were right, there would be no age group interested in seeing this movie. Oops, does this sound familiar? This was exactly what Mechanic had said before we ever started to make this picture.

My expectations were diminishing.

Wasn't marketing telling Mechanic that we were doomed from the start? Well, in a sense, that's right. The tacit communication from marketing goes something like this: 'You guys that "green-light" these movies and you guys that "make" these movies should have asked me first. I know what *they* want and what *they* don't want. But, since y'all didn't ask me, we here in marketing will do our level best to serve this turkey that you all cooked.' Since marketing is the last stop on the film's journey, the natural inclination is to not piss these marketing guys off.

So, once Harper gave his dire prognosis, I was eager to be polite and ooze gratitude. I thought I needed his support more than ever.

'Tell me what we should do, Bob.'

'Well, for starters, let's change that title . . .'

He was about to say *Bookworm*, but the word had become too distasteful.

'Sure, Bob, if that'll help.'

'That'll be a big help.'

'Hey, whatever works, you know me.'

I should have lost my producer's license with that remark.

For the next few weeks, while a trailer was being cut and different one sheets were being prepared, numerous lists of titles were made. Here were some of the choices:

Ambushed
To the Ambush
The Ambush
Wild
Wilder
The Wild
Into the Wild
Wilderness Now
Deadhunt
Deadfall
Precipice
On the Precipice
Over the Precipice
The Edge
Edge
On the Edge
The Bear Killer
The Bear Roared
The Bear and the Brain
Roared
Bloody Betrayal

At one time or another we had everything on this list but *If You Come to See This Shitstorm, We'll PAY YOU.*

I read the list to Mamet over the phone. When I finished, he was only able to utter, 'Oh, God.'

For those of you who saw this film on TV or happened to drift into your local cineplex, you know that we settled on *The Edge*. It's as if a committee of monkeys, of which I was a charter member, were trying to land a 747 in bad weather. Like most collective decisions made in the name of creativity, we ended up choosing a banal solution that would by definition be the least provocative and the least objectionable just to gain a consensus. Years later, I remain so dithered by the process that I can only refer to the film as 'the bear movie.'

Opening weekend, *The Edge* grossed $7.8 million in 2,150 screens, putting the movie in third position. No one from the studio called Tamahori or me with the news. The number one movie, *The Peacemaker*, grossed $12.3 million. Four weeks later, it became apparent that the domestic gross of our picture would settle around $30 million. Hardly a smash hit, and yet not a total wipeout. Compared to other recent Fox debacles such as *Firestorm, Newton Boys*, or *Chain Reaction*, we looked virginal.

When I saw Mechanic from my office window on the Tuesday following the opening, I was more than aware that we hadn't spoken since Friday. He was alone making the long trek from the administration building to the commissary, dwarfed by the kitschy murals painted on the sides of the large soundstages. As he passed under the sixty-foot-high rendering of Darth Vader dueling Luke Skywalker, I put all irony aside. I decided to intercept him and commiserate.

'Hey, Bill. How's it going?'

'It's lunchtime.'

'Sure is.'

He didn't look quite so sanguine up close.

'I know. I know. It's not a homer, but I'm thinking "ground rule double." '

'We're projecting the movie to lose ten million dollars,' he said stoically.

'Really.'

'That's right.'

'You know this even before it's released internationally?'

'That's right.'

'Even before the DVD comes out?'

'Pretty much.'

'What if—'

'Hear me, we're going to *lose money*.'

'I see.'

I assumed with that sort of forecast, Mechanic must be smarting from his own Murdoch/Chernin-inflicted rope burns.

We eyed each other, both of us awkwardly unfulfilled. Throughout the entire production, Bill had remained a supportive and generous influence. His disappointment was genuine. In the end, however, he was a victim and a slave to the numbers.

He kept walking.

I wanted to keep it cheery by adding, 'Say, Bill, maybe we can call it an "infield single"?'

But I decided to let it go.

SEVEN

GREAT EXPECTATIONS DASHED

'Didja know Mike makes the best margaritas in the city?'

'Jerry, everyone knows this.'

'Mike is a Czech bartender.'

'Uh-huh.'

'And Dan Tana is a Greek with a name change.'

'Yeah.'

'And Dan Tana's serves Italian food with margaritas.'

'There is a point here?'

'I believe there is.'

'What?'

'America is such a land of opportunity.'

'Jerry, your Zoloft is starting to kick in, and I think that's good.'

Mike had been pouring drinks at Tana's for almost thirty years. His hair dye was getting a little iffy, but all in all, he was holding up quite well considering that he'd seen everything pass by his bar, whether he'd wanted to or not. For Mike, serving a deposed studio head and an agitated producer was like watching grass grow.

Tana's seemed a perfect next stop for our sojourn. It had a bit of history to it. A makeshift red-and-white-checkered 'Italian' restaurant, Tana's catered nondiscriminatorily to anyone in the business. Always crowded, always tough to get a table, it remained a mainstay for those who were happening, for those who were no longer happening, and for those who would never happen. In the seventies, Nils Lofgren, currently Bruce Springsteen's guitar player, would enter the restaurant unannounced, laced on acid, and serenade the diners with an accordion while they were snorting coke at the tables. In the eighties, an erstwhile movie producer broke the jaw and nose of a literary agent over somebody else's wife. It was such a scene, it took months to get the agent's blood cleaned up from the carpeted floor. A producer and an agent spilling *real* blood could only happen at Tana's. In the nineties, all of those who were battle-scarred from the last two decades would gather at Tana's to recall the weirdness.

On the way to the restaurant, Jerry tried to convince me to go to the Palm instead.

'There's more pussy at the Palm,' he said.

'Jerry, this stuff we're doing is about something more than pussy.'

'I think we're capable of doing more than one thing at a time, don't you?'

'I'm paying.'

'That was our deal.'

'I choose.'

'Fine.'

Tana's seemed like the correct spot to continue our dialogue. I was feeling positive. Having Jerry's ear had somehow been therapeutic. And although he would never admit it, I could see he was beginning to feel as if he were back in the business. Over Jerry's shoulder, the legendary Lew Wasserman, in his late eighties, was seated with a group of people at the first corner booth. This was the guy who created Universal and MCA, the guy who once really ran the town, and he was just a few feet away. Jerry kept looking over. For a brief second they were facing each other before Wasserman stared back at his plate. I could tell that Jerry thought he had made a connection.

Excited by the prospect that Wasserman had acknowledged him, he nervously vibrated on his barstool. Jerry was from the generation that would still venerate a Wasserman. A nod from Lew was a kiss of Hollywood immortality. Unfortunately, Lew was getting on. He didn't have a clue. It was just an accidental gaze on his part, a momentary flick around the room while he was working hard to digest his food. I didn't want to blow it for Jerry, but Hollywood waits for no one, not even Wasserman.

Jerry handed me a package. A brown bag bound loosely with a rubber band.

'Don't say I never got you anything.'

'*Pour moi?* Why, Jerry?'

'Open it.'

Out slid an old edition of Charles Dickens's classic *Great Expectations*.

'You shouldn't of.'

'I found it on Melrose.'

He started to laugh in that annoying Richard Dreyfuss way, eh, eh eh.

'Jerry, I think I've read it.'

'Well, after I saw your movie of same name, I wasn't so sure.'

Now, he started to howl.

'Hey.'

'I was going to get you *War and Peace*,' he said while wiping the tears from his eyes, 'but in the spirit of preserving world order, I thought maybe I should keep you away from the Russians.'

He started banging the bar with his fists. Mike took it as a signal to bring him another margarita.

'Jerry, I admit that there was a lot of blood spilled on that movie, but some of it came out respectably.'

'Oh, let's not get touchy.'

'I'm not.'

'Of course you are.'

'No.'

'Indulge me. I had to listen to that drivel of you and Alec Baldwin arguing about *integrity*.'

'Is that a word you're unfamiliar with?'

'Hoo ha. Hoo ha,' Jerry again did an ugly imitation of Pacino's blind guy. '*Integrity!* My balls!' He grabbed his crotch with both hands.

'You know how to bring out the best in people.'

'I say, follow the money.'

'Jerry, I don't want you to throw up, but *some* of us have an ethical line we won't cross.'

'Follow the money.'

'Well, perhaps that's true too.'

'Male nurses at Cedars have integrity, but they don't get five million a picture, and God knows what Fox was paying you.'

I reddened.

'Were there any ideas you came up with that Fox didn't want to do?'

'Jerry, do you want me to continue or not?'

'Continue.'

'You're sure?'

'I'm sure.'

'Because if I caught you on a bad day, I'm happy to fuckin' leave.'

'I must say these stories are brightening my spirit.'

'Call me "surprised."'

The Wasserman party was slowly exiting. Dan Tana was genuflecting by the front door. I tried to suppress the thought that this might be Lew's last meal at Tana's. Jerry carefully eyed the group, hoping to exchange one more contact with the legend, but to no avail. If Lew did remember Jerry, he had certainly forgotten him by the time his dessert was finished. As the procession finally disappeared through the narrow archway, Jerry leaned over to Mike and asked politely if we could sit at Wasserman's table after it was cleared.

Mike obliged.

'When was the last time you looked at David Lean's *Great Expectations*?' John asked me. John was my son, who had been working with me at Warners and at Fox, reading scripts and supervising the development of some film projects.

'Twenty years,' I said.

'I just looked at it on television and it's great, you know, it's really great.'

'Of course, it's David Lean.'

'We should look at the book again.'

'Why?'

'It could be a terrific modern love story.'

'John, I've been down the Dickens road already, and it was punitive.'

'I know about *Scrooged*, but this would be different . . .'

'I can't.' I was resisting not only because of *Scrooged* but also because I was still selling the bear stuff to Fox and I didn't want to complicate things.

'You should look through the book. It wouldn't be a broad comedy, but it might make a great modern-day love story . . . poor young guy in love with the rich, pretty girl since childhood . . . always trying but never good enough to get her. Good stuff.'

'Shit.'

I knew it was a good idea, but I was already anticipating the huge boulders nestling in the center of the road.

From a producing point of view, John was right. Adapting and modernizing *Great Expectations* would be irresistible for a studio. First, it had a famous title. Studios love famous titles. I knew that when the marketing and development executives realized the movie already had a built-in awareness, they would get all warm and fuzzy, as if Murdoch had allowed them to have a glass of wine at lunch. Kind of like making a sequel. And they feasted on sequels. Second, Dickens had been dead for a long time. Couldn't we rob his grave and just take it? Well, of course, we could; it was in the public domain! It was free! We get a celebrated title and the underlying rights for nothing. Who could say no? All we would need is a good script and we were off.

I mentioned the idea to Bill Mechanic.

'Why not?'

'That's what I figured.'

'Run it by Jacobson.'

'I just went through this with Mamet. If I'm not mistaken, some of Mamet's undigested lunch is still on Tom's carpet.'

'C'mon, he's a good executive.'

'I can't help myself.'

'Who's going to write it?'

'I don't know yet.'

I spoke with John and we decided to talk to Mitch Glazer about the job. Actually, I asked Steve Zaillian (*Schindler's List, Awakenings*) first, but he declined. He muttered something about it being interesting but adapting Dickens seemed too daunting. Everyone asked Zaillian first. Mitch was the living half of the Michael O'Donoghue/Mitch Glazer team that had written the screenplay for *Scrooged*. He was also a close friend of mine. Before we get into the instructional saga of how friendships are profoundly affected by the wrenching pressures of filmmaking, let's just say that Mitch's first marriage took place at my house, he's known John since childhood, and we all worked blissfully together on *Scrooged*.

In November 1994, Michael O'Donoghue pissed everybody off by dying suddenly of a brain aneurysm. His head burst. The darkly brilliant wit, whose gutsy humor had defined and launched *SNL*, was an original. Famous for creating sketches such as Gilda Radner singing, "So, let's kill Gary Gilmore for Christmas,' he and Mitch became a formidable writing team and created some authentically brutal cinema comedy. The tone of their screenplay for Dickens's *Christmas Carol* was irreverent and very funny. Starring Bill Murray as the mean-spirited network executive Frank (Scrooge) Cross, here's a small sample of their approach:

INT. AREA OUTSIDE FRANK'S OFFICE – DAY
Frank (Murray) and Grace (his secretary) reach Grace's desk, neat and impersonal save for a child's finger painting taped to her cubicle wall.

FRANK
And, Grace, would you ah . . . oh,
What's the name of the kid I was just
talking to? With glasses, bright, lots of guts?

GRACE
Eliot Loudermilk.

FRANK
Would you call security, have them clean out his
desk, change his locks, and toss him out of the
building.

GRACE
He's fired? But it's Christmas.

FRANK
Thank you. Call accounting and have his
bonus stopped.

GRACE
(on phone)
Loudermilk? Code Nine.

FRANK
What's this?

GRACE
It's a painting one of my kids did. See, there's
Santa and . . .

FRANK
How many fingers does Mrs. Claus have on
her left hand?

GRACE
(studying it)
Four.

FRANK
On her right?

GRACE
Seven.

He yanks it off the wall and tosses it to her.

FRANK
Grace, it's crap. Lose it.

He heads for his office. Grace takes out the Christmas list.

FRANK

Okay, let's get this over with. Read me the list.

GRACE

Goldberg.

FRANK

Send him a VHS home video recorder.

GRACE

Parker.

FRANK

VHS.

GRACE

Kaluta.

FRANK

The bath towel.

GRACE

Brock.

FRANK

Towel.

GRACE

Whiteacre.

FRANK

What was the last rating on *Police Zoo*?

GRACE

Five point two Nielsen, seven share, and a TVQ of three.

FRANK/GRACE

(together)

Towel.

GRACE

Your brother.

FRANK

Towel.

Mitch agreed to take on *Great Expectations*, but with some trepidation. We all knew that the tone of this screenplay would have to be completely different from *Scrooged*. There would be no irascible asshole to set off, no hard laughs to deflect the audience. This Dickensian tale was a one-sided kismet love story; it had to be taken seriously. Even if O'Donoghue could have contributed, we still couldn't escape with a bent comedy. The approach would have to be grounded in the reality and sentiment of the book or it would become a laughable sketch. And just as worrying, if the movie was to be done seriously, it would inevitably be compared to the David Lean classic. And who wants to stand the gaff for that. Knowing all that, Mitch cinched his belt, took the money, and decided to give it a go.

'It's Tom Jacobson.'

'What's his deal?' Mitch asked.

'Just below Mechanic on the food chain.'

'Does he have the power to say no?'

'Hard to tell.'

'He knows the idea, right?'

'Yeah, says he's a fan of yours.'

'That's nice.'

'We're going to meet him in the commissary.'

'It's better than the office, don't ya think?'

'Makes it smoother, less like a "pitch" meet.'

'Great.'

'Anyway, Mechanic seems in for the idea.'

'I think I'm ready.'

Mitch and I were making that long walk down the cement lane to the commissary. It was 12:45 P.M. As the throngs fled from their offices, I was again saddled with the image that the central headquarters for Aetna insurance had just broken for lunch. Despite the vain attempts at displaying Hollywood memorabilia, the ghosts of Hollywood past were long gone from Fox. Call me sentimental, but I was always hoping to get a glimpse of Darryl Zanuck sneaking some starlet through a private door.

Mitch, like most writers, hated to pitch. Writing is about rewriting, and when you're 'pitching,' there's little chance to retrace your steps and make it 'sound' better if things are beginning to skid off course. With this in mind, we had spent the last several days discussing the specifics. Even though we were about to have a casual lunch, we both knew it was essential to be ready.

These meetings were always greatly unpredictable. You could never bet on the outcome. Years ago at Universal, I wanted to make a rock-and-roll bio pic of the famed disc jockey Alan Freed. I had just produced the hit movie *Car Wash*, and I assumed that the next thing I pitched to them would be met with gratitude. After all, once you've sold 'a day in the life of a car wash put to music,' and it dumbfoundedly worked, you figured that Hollywood was a cakewalk. I thought if I burped, they'd buy it. I went to see Ned Tanen, then head of motion pictures for Universal, and the guy who had bought *Car Wash*.

As the elevator door opened on the penultimate floor of the black tower, you turned to face a floating staircase that led to the very top floor. Presumably, this was reserved for the founder, Jules Styne. Mortals were not permitted up there. One sensed that after Styne had departed his body, the space would be held exclusively for guardian angels. On either side of the staircase were offices that housed Lew Wasserman, Sid Sheinberg, and Ned Tanen. The colorless solemnity of the place worked on your confidence. When you were finished with your business, they were going to remain there and you weren't.

Years later it took Michael Ovitz and I. M. Pei to top this sort of hubris. They concocted the hideous marble and glass mausoleum for CAA, in the heart of Beverly Hills, which is even more foreboding and less generous than the black tower. The building was designed to punish. So sweaty in its need to express power, it inadvertently overwhelms the visitor. The lobby witlessly screams, 'We're big, we're significant, we're indestructible . . . you're not.' Smothered and diminished by a silly oversize Lichtenstein and vast hard-edged walls reaching toward the skylight, you awkwardly crane your neck upward hoping someone will rescue you from the marble pit and mercifully lead you to a smaller office. Usually you are compelled to wait while you are stared at from glass hallways by a multitude of carefully dressed agents and business-affairs people perched several floors above. They conveniently 'look down' to see who's there. You are soon convinced that some important shit must be happening in this building (CIA or Pentagon stuff) because all this grave pomp and circumstance couldn't possibly be about *show business*. Not surprisingly, it seems to have had an equally stultifying effect on the agents who worked there every day. It's just a building, of course, but the DNA of it has unwittingly shackled decent guys with a big debt and the arrogant legacy of their predecessor. Some of them in the last few years have banged into the walls so fiercely that they were never heard from again. I guess if Ovitz's aim was to create a lot of space, he forgot the oxygen.

Okay. I don't know what just got hold of me, but I feel better now.

The solemnity of the fourteenth floor of Universal's black tower was not eased when Tanen saw me exit the elevator. He motioned for me to come into his office. I had to remind myself that I was coming off a hit. People were still humming the theme from *Car Wash* in the halls. I didn't have to wait. I was entitled.

'Okay, let me have it,' he said.

'The beginning of rock and roll.'

'Yeah?'

'Alan Freed.'

'Yeah?'

'How the music affected the kids.'

My mind was going blank. I realized I hadn't really worked out the story. I guess I hadn't thought I needed to. Tanen leaned back and put his feet up on the desk. He was vaguely amused by my sputtering, but I would have had to have produced *Jaws* for him to nibble on this performance.

'And the story?'

'Well, we take a close look at Freed and payola and it culminates in a big rock-and-roll show at the end.'

'Uh-huh.'

'I gotta work more on the details.'

'I'll get back to you.'

A week later I got word that Tanen had passed. So much for being too clever. I spent the next month with John Kaye, the screenwriter, detailing the story. This time I went to Paramount. As it worked in Hollywood, the goodwill that I had received from *Car Wash*'s success generated some traction at Paramount, even though the hit was for another studio. Success was contagious. With a more specific plan worked out, they purchased the pitch, hired Kaye, and the movie *American Hot Wax* resulted. A footnote to this meeting is that Michael Eisner and Don Simpson were the young executives at Paramount who loved the pitch. When I finished my spiel, they winked at each other. I guess the lesson here is to be prepared. Is that lesson ever learned?

The hostess in the Fox commissary led Mitch and me to a table conspicuously in the center of a packed room. We were seated across from Jacobson, who had been waiting. He was clear-eyed and well rested, nothing splotchy about Tom. Mel Brooks was seated three tables away.

'I love Dickens,' Jacobson said.

'Everybody loves Dickens,' I blurted out.

'My favorite book in college,' he added.

'My favorite book in high school,' I countered.

I tried to get a grip, but after that Mamet pitch, Tom brought out the best in me. I knew I wasn't making it easy for anyone. I put my hand on Tom's shoulder, attempting to assuage my sarcasm. He moved inches to his left, not welcoming the physical contact. Who could blame him? Couldn't we just play by the rules? Tom was supposed to be having lunch with a screenwriter and a producer to size up the efficacy of modernizing Dickens. Mitch and I were supposed to do our parts and try to sell him. Simple enough, which was why Jacobson was probably wondering why I was making this so damn complicated.

'So, Mitch, go 'head. What's the modern version?' Tom asked.

Not to belabor the story, but Mitch went on to explain that this version of *Great Expectations* would begin on Florida's Gulf Coast and end up in New York City. Instead of young Pip trying to get accepted as a nineteenth-century gentleman in London society, our Pip was going to escape the poverty of a fishing village and try to get accepted as a celebrated artist. His trying to survive the Dickensian coincidences that continually tugged at his life would be modernized. The underlying tale of Pip trying to get the girl who was beyond his reach, to shed his modest past while getting help from a secret benefactor, would remain intact.

In the Dickens story, Pip, once accepted for his new success, gets visited by his poor uncle who raised him. Embarrassed by his past, he regrettably humiliates his uncle. In the drama, it is the Dickensian moment when the main character hits bottom. The character has to become an asshole before he can be redeemed.

'I really like the new setting,' Tom said.

'We like it too,' Mitch said.

'Fisherman to artist,' Tom said.

'Good stuff,' I said.

'The benefactor turns out to be an escaped convict, I like it,' Tom continued.

'Don't forget Estella, the beautiful girl damaged by her rich past,' I said.

'I didn't.'

'Is there something else you need to know?' Mitch asked.

'Mitch, are you concerned that when Pip embarrasses his uncle, he becomes an unlikable character?'

'Huh?' Mitch was getting edgy.

'Well, would the audience still root for him?'

Déjà vu. Mitch looked at me with moist eyes, wondering how seriously he was supposed to take this remark. I'd been there before, so I was no help.

'What do you mean "root"?' I asked.

'Well, you know, we want the audience to pull for him, not against him.'

In Tom's defense, he is not alone. His apprehension about pandering to audiences is shared by almost every executive in Hollywood. It's in the nature of their jobs to decide what the 'great unwashed' want and what they don't want, and there is no handbook to guide them. This invariably leads to the false conclusion that if an audience is momentarily upset with a character or with the direction of a story, they will not ultimately embrace the movie. Even though the executives know of so many exceptions, from *Taxi Driver* to *The Shining*, where audiences lined up for movies that were not designed to be 'nice,' for some reason, perhaps simply a lack of true vision, they weaken when the story makes a nonconforming turn.

Every filmmaker in Hollywood will evenutally have to deal with this situation. It's the producer's job, in assisting the writer and the director, to prevent those who are spending the money from negatively affecting crucial creative decisions. Sometimes sidestepping the issue is the good plan. Sometimes stonewalling the issue is a better plan.

'Pip is one of the most beloved characters in English literature,' Mitch said.

'Everybody loves Pip,' I added.

'I love Pip, I just want you guys to be aware that this could be a problem.'

At that moment, Mel Brooks, who was making the rounds while giving each table twenty seconds of spritz, came to our table and said, 'So, what kinda movie are you boys cooking up?'

We all said in unison, *'Great Expectations.'*

'Sounds good, boys, sounds good.' He muttered something about *The Elephant Man*, a movie that he had produced for Fox years ago, and then drifted away. The lunch was over.

EIGHT

A GLASS JAW

'**S**he has no chin.'

'Come again?'

'She has no chin.'

Tom Rothman was talking from behind his desk. I was sitting next to Alfonso Cuarón on Rothman's couch. Cuarón, a newcomer to this sort of Hollywood madness, looked over at me incredulously.

'But . . . I theenk Gwyneth ess beauuutiful,' Alfonso said.

'I'm not going to cast her,' Rothman said, trying his damnedest to look empathetic.

We had just received word from Gwyneth Paltrow's agent that she wanted to do the movie. Cuarón and I were excited to have her, but at this point in her career, she wasn't a household name. I had first become aware of Gwyneth from her small roles in *Flesh and Bone* and *Se7en*. She had yet to grace the covers of every magazine in the world, and I believe it was even before anyone knew she was sleeping with Brad Pitt. Nonetheless, the heat was on. Most savvy insiders knew that she was a 'comer' and a promising addition to any cast. She was already in demand, already hard to get. And most of all, for the part of Estella, the unattainable, beautiful ice princess who has been taught not to love, Gwyneth with her ease and sophistication was perfect casting.

'She has no chin,' Rothman persisted.

'But, I really like her cheeen.'

Alfonso was a young director born and reared in Mexico City, who had made his American directorial debut with the critically acclaimed *A Little Princess* for Warner Bros. Although the movie did not perform particularly well at the box office, Cuarón's work had a bold, magical quality that had size and heart. This director had some significant talent, and he was being courted by most of the studios.

Several months after pitching the idea and concluding the negotiations, Glazer finished a few drafts of *Great Expectations*. We agreed that it was ready to turn in to Fox, where it was strongly supported by Bill Mechanic, Rothman's superior. Fortunately, the script had made a sufficient enough impact at Fox for them to let me go fishing and see what elements it would attract. I had sent the script to several directors preapproved by Mechanic and Rothman. This does not mean they were obligated to make the movie with these directors, but it did mean that they would at least start the dialogue. As the script began to circulate through the Hollywood pipeline, many directors shied away from the material, apparently reluctant to take on a movie based on a classic. After about a month, I received a call from Alfonso's agent, Steve Rabineau. He said Cuarón had just called him from Europe, that he had some real interest, and that he wanted to call me with some questions. At this point, Alfonso and I had never met.

'*Great Expectations* is my very favorite film,' he said on the phone.

'I'm so glad.'

'I love that film.'

'Me too.'

'But . . .'

'Maybe we should wait till you return from Portugal.'

'No, ess okay to do it now.'

'Okay.'

'But, you see that is also the problem.'

'A problem with the old film?'

'Yes, I love it *too* much.'

'It's David Lean, isn't it?'

'That ees correct.'

'How can we overcome this?'

'Well, I have seen many of your movies . . .'

'Well, thank you.'

'And I notice you get to spend lots and lots of money.'

'Uh-huh.'

'Are you going to get me lots of money to make this movie?'

'Gosh, I'm gonna try.'

'Do you promise to try very hard?'

'I promise.'

'Good, I like that.'

Actually, this was a good question to ask. As disarming as Alfonso was, he was also smart. He knew that to compete with the past, this version would require some extravagant moves to set it apart. Unlike, let's say, *Clueless*, which was a well-executed spoof version of Jane Austen's *Emma*, our script was attempting to take the underlying Dickens text seriously and therefore would and should be judged by audiences and critics as a serious film. Alfonso liked the script, but he said, as almost all directors do when they first commit to something, that it needed more work. He was looking forward to working with Mitch and me when he returned to Hollywood, and he was eager to give it a go. Instead of sensing any red flags, I was charmed by him. In fact, I thought many of his concerns were well founded. I liked that he was thinking big. And who doesn't want to 'deepen' the characters? Mechanic and Rothman, because of the promise of *A Little Princess*, were happy to have landed him. A deal was concluded for Alfonso to helm the picture, but the contract was subject to budget, subject to cast, and subject to script changes. In fact, if one were to riffle through the fine print, it was probably subject to the weather. This meant Fox was still flirting. This deal was as solid as a fat man's first attempt on a skateboard.

'She's not a star; it's not going to work,' Rothman persisted.

Cuarón, dismayed, but trying hard to hold on, leaned forward and motioned to me for help. 'Come on, you're the producer. Do something!' I'd been there before. I wasn't too worried. With English as a second language, and without knowing Rothman personally, Alfonso must have been struggling to get a bead on this sort of wacky behavior. Since replacing Jacobson, Rothman had seemed to dive into his new role as someone who insisted on telling you (and at great length) what he *thought*. With his newfound power, he had thoughts on just about everything.

I didn't want to break Rothman's piñata, but as he would eventually learn, his particular job description was to be 'keeper of the sequels.' This meant he was hired to make sure that filmmakers who had provided Fox with past hits would be persuaded to keep the flame going by making hit sequels. Fox had a vast pot to choose from. There was *Planet of the Apes, Independence Day, Speed, Star Wars, Alien, French Connection*, etc. If Tom wanted his back slapped by upper management, he should have been spending his time getting someone to remake those titles. It's a big bullet to bite, but he was not hired to cast movies, write movies, direct movies, or even produce movies. He was a businessman.

This sort of behavior was not new. It was like a viral infection. When executives are given their first blush of power, it's like an itch that has to be scratched. The need to throw their weight around and act 'creative' is simply irresistible. Like most infections, either it clears up with time or else it kills you. These types of stories have been repeating themselves since the studio system began. Years ago, as the folklore goes, when Herb Ross wanted Kevin Bacon to star in *Footloose*, Dawn Steel, the newly appointed production head at Paramount, shrieked, 'Don't want to fuck him. Can't cast him. I just don't want to fuck him!' Word has it, she learned this from Don Simpson, who, if he objected to a casting choice male or female, would always say, 'I wouldn't fuck him with your dick.' Rothman, not in this legendary company, was unready to talk about intercourse.

'Tom, we really, *really* like her,' I said with a strong enough tone that indicated we could talk about this, but that Cuarón and I might not be prepared to make the movie without her. Anyway, her already beautiful chin was going to look a lot better to Rothman once she acquired fame.

'I theeenk she ess fantastic.'

'Well, let me think about it.'

'Good,' I added. 'She has several job offers and we have to move quickly.'

Once a movie script starts to get a foothold at a studio, the momentum must be maintained. A producer must always remember that nobody 'needs' to make a movie. If the studio heads give it too much thought, they could easily change their minds. If you think about it, these executives are about to provide a group of people, whom they barely like, with *thirty million dollars* to make a movie. This could turn out to be a truly funky mistake. At this stage, as much as I wanted to dive over Tom's desk, grab him, place my knee firmly on his chest, and scream, 'YOU'RE AN INSANE CHUCK-LEHEAD! THIS GIRL IS GOING TO BE ON THE COVER OF *VOGUE* AND WIN AN OSCAR. GO TAKE A FUCKING SHOWER,' I knew violent acts would not be rewarded. There was a delicate balance here, and it had to be prolonged until a green light was firmly in place. For me, resolutely pushing forward was the only mantra.

'*I* can't make this movie without a star,' Rothman said. Little white flecks of foam were forming on the corners of his mouth.

Another odd tic that occurs when an executive is given the

sweatshirt of authority is the use of the word *I* instead of *you* or even *we* when referring to the making of movies. To be fair, this astonishing exhibition of self-confusion was not limited to Rothman. In fact, it's rare to find an executive these days who will not say things like 'Two years ago when *I made* [fill in the famous title of your choice] blah blah blah.' Directors and writers, who actually do the prodigious work for these guys, have to patiently listen to this drivel with their eyes glazed over waiting to pick up the money. Executives simply confuse making a committee business decision with making a movie. I think it makes them feel artsy.

'Maybe we can find a star to play a cameo?' I asked.

'Like who?'

'What about Robert De Niro to play the convict.'

Alfonso grinned. I thought he was about to jump up and say, 'Olé.'

'I *like* Bobby,' Rothman declared.

Bobby. Bobby! A minute before getting this job, Rothman would have been saying, 'Mr De Niro, can I please freshen your drink?' Now, even though they had never met, he was already calling him 'Bobby.'

He couldn't help himself. This kind of congenital weirdness gets distributed with the parking space on the Fox lot. As time went on for Rothman, and the attendant pressures of the job expanded, things would start to even out. Insecurities and disappointments would erode the confidence of the most successful of these executives. After some of my movies came out, particularly the ones that were not successful, Rothman's behavior took a strange bent. He began to remind me of a guy standing uncomfortably at his desk with the barrel of a .357 Magnum pressed tightly to his temple, threatening everyone in the room, 'If you come any closer, *I* am going to pull the trigger.'

You remember six months earlier, when I was talking to Robert

De Niro at the Peninsula Hotel about doing *The Edge* and he had some major concerns about acting with a mechanical bear? Well, undaunted and in the best tradition of Sammy Glick, I rolled up my other sleeve and revealed a different kind of timepiece that might catch his eye.

'You remember *Great Expectations*?'

'Why?'

'I'm just asking, do you remember *Great Expectations*?'

'I think so.'

'The Dickens thing.'

'Of course, I know.'

'Do you remember the convict who ends up being the benefactor?'

'Vaguely, I think so.'

'Well . . .'

'Well what?'

'Oh. We're developing it into a modern-day movie.'

'Good.'

'The convict's gonna be a great part.'

'It doesn't have a bear in it, does it?'

'No bear.'

'I might get interested.'

'How interested.'

'How many days?'

'I don't know, the script isn't done yet.'

'How many days do you think?'

'Well, it's a substantial cameo, goes throughout the movie.'

'How many days?'

Bob was trying to find out if the studio would be willing to compress the convict's schedule. This means shooting all of the scenes with the convict consecutively, then interspersing those scenes throughout the film during the editing. The advantage to Bob would be that he could get all of his work done in a short time and still make the same amount of money. Maybe, he would have time to fit in another movie while this one was still shooting. This can put great strain on the production. By shooting out of sequence, the ability to change things that might not work is always compromised. Sets and locations often have to be duplicated. It often adds considerable costs to the overall budget. Nonetheless, if you want or need an actor badly enough, you learn to dance on a pinhead. Based on my preliminary meetings with Fox, I knew that we were going to need De Niro or somebody else just as significant.

'Who knows, if we compress the convict's schedule, maybe seven to nine days.'

'Seven days. I could get very interested.'

'Really?'

'Yeah.'

From Bob this was almost a commitment. I was tempted to do something foolish like say 'We're not going to need a read-through on this one, are we?' But, I sensed that for whatever made him tick, *Great Expectations* was something that would fit into his master plan. I knew I was one big step closer to getting a movie made.

I'd like to say that Ethan Hawke was my first choice for Pip, that I saw all his movies and loved them, that I fought the studio like a producer with great integrity, and that finally, against all odds, I got them to commit to the underdog. Not the case. John and I would spend endless hours going over wish lists, but the pickings were slim. We were hoping for Brad Pitt or even Keanu Reeves, but they turned us down flat. Many of the young actors out there who were excellent and who had sufficient standing to help us get the movie financed were not responding. When I got the call from Bryan Lourd at CAA that Ethan was willing, I was relieved. I knew that Ethan was enough of an actor on the rise to stimulate Fox, especially with the spice that De Niro's flirtation provided. John and I had some concerns, but after so many turndowns, it was no longer time to focus on artistic chemistry. I had shifted into full producer mode: Let's get this movie made no matter what. Ethan was a good actor. Trying to marshal all of my optimism, I thought maybe he could carry the movie.

I kept De Niro current with the progress of the script, and meanwhile, he did his homework. Bob always did his homework. He saw the David Lean movie. He read through the Dickens book. When the script was ready, he read it and reconfirmed his enthusiasm. One last hurdle. I waited anxiously for Bob to come out of the screening of *A Little Princess*, knowing he had to approve of Alfonso.

'What do you think?'

'Uh . . . seven days is good.'

NINE

I'M DRIVING A PINTO

S arasota, Florida, is particularly hot in July. When you have less money to spend on a movie than your director wants to spend, it feels even hotter. I made several proclamations before we started filming. I told Alfonso that I would get him lots of money to make this movie. I told Bill Mechanic that we could do this movie in sixty-two days and we would stay on budget. I told Alfonso, who wanted more work on the script as the start date neared, that Mitch would be available and willing to accommodate him and that we could get this work done *while* we were shooting. Disagreements or artistic differences would be no problem; I would be there to referee. When Ethan Hawke said that he also had script concerns, I smiled and told him we welcomed his input. When the cinematographer, Emmanuel Lubezki *(A Little Princess, Birdcage, Sleepy Hollow)*, nicknamed Chivo, registered much concern about the size of his lighting package and the pace of the schedule, I told him not to worry. We would find a way to make it all work. Also born and raised in Mexico, Chivo, who looked like an under-nourished Kenny G, was, like his childhood amigo, a 'perfectionist.' No matter how good things were going, he always had that hapless expression 'You're killing me, can't you see, you're killing me.' You know where this is going. Somebody was going to get pissed off. Maybe everybody.

Perfectionist is a nasty word. I remember when Michael Mann was in the middle of shooting *Heat*. He had just completed the bank robbery sequence in downtown Los Angeles, which had taken longer to film than any other bank robbery in the history of cinema. We were desperately over schedule. Arnon Milchan, one of the investors with Warner Bros., came to the set with his entourage to try to convince Michael to pick up the pace. While we were waiting in Mann's trailer for him to break for lunch, Arnon asked me if there was anything in the schedule that Michael could shorten to get back on time. 'Gosh, I don't know, Arnon; you know Michael, he's a *perfectionist*.' The mere use of the word made the entire group physically ill. Even I felt a little shaky. While to some it might have conjured up unyielding artistic integrity, to the bank it screamed, 'I don't understand the word *compromise*. Secure your knee pads.' Michael entered the trailer. Arnon repeated his plea while Michael quietly listened. He even occasionally nodded with concern for Arnon's predicament. Finally Michael stood up, looked at his watch, and said, 'I'm afraid lunch is only thirty minutes. If I don't get back now, we're going to fall *another* day behind.'

The temperature in southwest Florida was in the nineties and the air was thick with humidity. Alfonso and I were standing in front of the large Venetian Gothic mansion, Ca d'Zan, on Sarasota Bay, which was going to serve as our primary location. This imposing structure had lavish gardens and a slightly nutty touch, probably because it was built by one of the circus Ringling brothers. Over the last ten years it has remained a minor tourist attraction for the dispossessed. For our purposes, the location was to serve as the crumbling estate of Ms. Dinsmoor, the eccentric rich aunt of Estella (Gwyneth). The descriptive line in the script read, '*Paradiso Perduto* [the name of the crumbling estate] is the land that time forgot.' Alfonso took this line seriously. He spent tens of thousands of dollars transforming the well-kept structure and the meticulous gardens into twenty years of dilapidated rot. Following the script, remnants of a wedding that had never taken place were now decaying in a vast garden covered with dead palm fronds and overgrown brush. All that was missing were live rats, but they were on order.

'Come here, I want to show you the wedding cake,' Alfonso said excitedly as we walked through the maze of the garden. He was content. He had finally snagged De Niro for the convict, cast Anne Bancroft for the eccentric aunt, and added two wonderful actors, Hank Azaria and Chris Cooper, to join Hawke and Paltrow. Glazer was turning out different variations on the script. And we were spending money at a furious pace, trying to keep up with his imagination. It was getting tight.

As we sidestepped a grand piano encrusted in mud, leaning awkwardly against a busted bandstand, I said, 'I think you've just about done it, don't you?'

'Ees going to be great, I think, huh?'

'I think it's great now.'

'Don't worry, we're almost there.'

Two women and a man all dressed identically in khaki Bermuda shorts strolled on the grounds taking photographs. One of the crew motioned for them to stop, and as they started to walk away, the man turned to us, held his nose, and said disappointedly, 'Boy, they've really let this place go downhill, haven't they?'

We both nodded and smiled.

'See, it's making *them* sick. I think we're there,' I said.

It was a couple of weeks before we were to start photography, and considering that costs were already bursting, the mood from Fox was remarkably quiet. I soon learned why we seemed to be flying under the radar. A month and a half before we started photography, *Titanic* began filming. The scale and the costs of that movie were so immense that until we got into real trouble, no one at Fox paid any attention to us. We were the little Negro stepchild who occasionally needed another pair of shoes, while the other kid was off building a nuclear bomb. When the name James Cameron was uttered above a whisper, Mechanic, Rothman, et al. would jerk their heads upward and downward as if they were jolted by a fire drill. When we completed the first eight days of shooting, we were already a week behind schedule, and no one from Fox had even called us.

Let me take an ugly left turn for a moment, if for no other reason but to keep both of us enthused. Mechanic and Rothman didn't tell Cuarón or me that a pivotal scene in *Titanic* – one that centered the entire romance in the film – was identical to one in our movie. Whether it was a grand coincidence or an accidental stealing or something even darker, I don't know. Both main characters were burgeoning young artists hired by the rich girl to be drawn nude, resulting in love, romance, and sex. We never saw the *Titanic* script, but if you look at both movies, it would be clear that Fox had to hold our little movie from release until the monster drank first. If we had anything fresh to offer, it was preempted. We were steamrolled.

By the time we were in release, critics, and no doubt half the paying audience, were commenting that this must be the year of the young artist who paints his girlfriend naked. But since we didn't have enough money, or the inclination, to sink an ocean liner, this love story was our best shot, our only shot. By the time *Great Expectations* was seen, *Titanic* had already grossed five hundred million dollars. I admit that the big boat going down was their denouement. Nonetheless, when Gwyneth removes her shoes, unhooks her bra, slides off her panties, and asks a twittering Ethan, 'Do you want me standing or sitting?' what else could the audience feel but 'been there, done that.' We were as fresh as an *I Love Lucy* rerun.

'What sort of twisted logic would get you to compare *Titanic* to whatever you're doing?' Jerry asked.

'There was a run on young artists as a theme. No one told us.'

'Get over it.'

'That's what I'm trying to do.'

'Oh, boy.'

'What?'

'A movie producer that pretends, oh, that's good.'

'Facts are facts, Jerry.'

'I believe you're taking this whole thing too personal.'

'That's very accurate.'

'Weren't you the one that said a producer is merely the mayonnaise?'

'Well, thank you for remembering.'

'Mayonnaise!?'

'That was a long time ago.'

'What exactly—'

'It means we're supposed to—'

'I know what't means.'

'Supposed to make things go more smoothly.'

'I think your exact words were, "Producers are the *mayonnaise* between the talent and the money on the way to making a *shit* sandwich."'

'Not exactly how I put it, Jerry.'

'Do you know what happens when you leave mayonnaise out in the *sun?*'

'Gosh, let me guess . . . it goes off,' I uttered, continuing to be Laurel to his Hardy.

'If I were you, I'd be spending more time in the *shade.*'

That made him laugh. I took a big gulp of the Chianti.

'My God, don't they serve hard liquor here?' he asked.

'Only wine.'

We were seated in the center of Giorgio's, a small Italian restaurant located at the mouth of the Santa Monica Canyon across from the Pacific Coast Highway. Sandwiched between a gay bar and a bikini shop, Giorgio's is a tiny hot spot that caters to the famous and tries its best to cater to the less than famous. The waiter, reminiscent of Joe Pesci down on his luck, had just brought the obligatory free starter of shaved octopus with steamed potato. While he started to run through the specials, Jerry, now in rare form, was mocking the waiter with macho Italian hand gestures. Actually, I'm not sure what he was doing. He grabbed his balls with his left hand, stiffened his right forearm, and made a fist. I guess Jerry was getting a bit too heady from sitting at such a prime table. Even Giorgio waved to him from the kitchen, figuring that he must be somebody. Jerry was so splendidly out of the loop that his eccentricities seemed comical. I indulged him.

'Don'tcha think,' Jerry said, 'the water level for producers is getting irrepressibly low?'

'You may be right.'

'Mind if I'm direct?'

'Do I have a choice?'

'If you didn't have Bob De Niro's home phone number, you might not have much of a producing career.'

'Oh, that's gone too far.'

'Hey, according to you, you'd send a script about an all-girls school to De Niro. What's with that?'

'Excuse me?'

'You think you'd get that masterpiece of yours made if you only had Joe Mantegna's number?'

'Bob was good casting.'

'Who cares?'

'It was an artistic choice.'

'Oh, let's not go artistic again.'

'What would you call it, Jerry?'

'Desperation.'

'I think not.'

'What happened to the producer's motto "I saw, I conquered, I *came*."'

'We've grown up.'

'Hoo haa. Hoo haa.'

There he goes again with that bad Pacino imitation, and again he started banging the table trying to control himself. Elena, Giorgio's daughter, who ran the room, looked over, concerned. She backed off when I held up my hand indicating that all was cool. This was going to be a long night. I was suddenly feeling a pang of regret that I didn't do drugs anymore. I had to pace myself. Anyway, Jerry's credibility was in the margins. That caustic bastard. He was burnt. Hell, there was a lot more to this producing thing than just getting 'Bobby' on the phone. Wasn't there?

The grind had begun.

I was on a plane returning from Canmore, Canada, to Miami, Florida. It was my third trip in the last four weeks. I had just gone through the horrendous beard incident with Alec Baldwin, and my nerves were brittle. I had waved good-bye, leaving Baldwin clean-shaven, fat, and pissed off, and Lee Tamahori unsettled—although they both had Elle Macpherson around for company. That's right, if you've been paying attention, both *The Edge* (that bear movie) and *Great Expectations* were shooting at the same time. This required a lot of traveling and a lot of accommodating.

The thunderstorms in Miami forced air traffic control to keep us spinning and bouncing for an extra hour before landing. I soon found out that it mirrored what was happening on the ground. Over the last few weeks, with the pressure building, Alfonso was getting racked. When filming was going well and dailies looked fine, he was excited and motivated. When things got rocky, he got rocky. When you're in the middle of the stampede, and you're a new director, all kinds of monsters can surface. Usually, the director gets sick during filming and has to work with the flu for several weeks. In that sort of weakened state, directors are manageable. It was too soon to know how Alfonso was going to fare, but his health was fine. As the plane jerked on the tarmac, I had the ugly recognition that the real 'tough' stuff hadn't even begun.

The initial problems on the set were minor and typical. Chivo and Alfonso were having a hard time getting the day's work done and were blaming it on weather, sun, shadows, and of course, not enough money or time. That first week of shooting is a shakedown cruise. It is always a bit unpredictable how the crew, the director, and the cast are going to mesh. Sometimes it takes a week or two for the machinery to run smoothly. When I arrived on the set, Cuarón and Chivo were huddled off to one side speaking Spanish. They would speak Spanish to each other when frustrations peaked, and they would speak English when things were going swell. When I saw John, he told me that they hadn't spoken English with each other for three days.

'We have to find a way to go faster,' I said.

'But the light ees killing us.'

'We're behind—'

'I know, I know.'

'But we haven't even burnt film on our stars yet.'

'That's a good thing, no?'

'No, it isn't a good thing.'

Our schedule required that we start with Gwyneth's and Ethan's characters when they first met as ten-year-old children. For those of you who saw the film, it included those scenes where the boy was first smitten, when they had their first kiss by the fountain, etc. Usually, when your principal actors are working, things will go even slower, and that we were already falling behind was a bit concerning. Even though Fox was leaving us alone for now, we would certainly have to pay the price at the end of the schedule. Important things that we would need down the road would be compromised. I didn't want to waste all of our extra time on the first week of shooting. It was difficult to explain this to Alfonso because he was knee-deep in the heat of battle.

'It rains, then it suns; it rains, then it suns.'

'It's Florida,' I said.

'The script needs more work.'

'Mitch is here to work on it.'

'Maybe we need more money.'

'We just started.'

'You said when we first talked that we would have lots of money.'

'We do have lot . . .'

'Maybe we need more.'

'Maybe we can't get more.'

'Well, I thought we would be driving a Rolls-Royce.'

'What are we driving?'

'A Pinto.'

This wasn't as scary as it sounded. The dailies looked magnificent. The performances as well as the photography were a cut above. Cuarón was quickly exhibiting the skills of a good director. I was sure that his worries would recede as the production continued.

The Dickensian name of Pip was discarded early by Mitch, who renamed him Pompi in the earliest of his drafts. Cuarón, who struggled with the name Pompi, got Mitch to change it to Jimmy. Ethan, who had been prepping in Florida for several weeks, and who was deliberating over the 'right' wig to make him look sixteen for the early scenes, was also concerned with the 'right' name for his character. When Ethan started rehearsals, he didn't like either name. He told us he was going to work on it. Two days before photography began, Ethan decided the character's name had to be changed to Finn. No one particularly liked this choice (I truly hated it) but, call it jet lag, pathetic capitulation to your lead actor, or being distracted by other problems, we decided to go with Finn. I heard later that it was the name of a dog that Ethan had had when he was growing up in Texas.

Weeks later, things got worse. I called Mitch in the middle of one of his rewrites to tell him that I had just seen Ethan's wig.

'What did you think?'

'It ain't making him look younger.'

'That's not good.'

'It's got that queasy look to it.'

'What do you mean?'

'It makes him look like a recovering cancer victim.'

'Did you tell him?'

'I was subtle, I grimaced.'

'Did he notice?'

'No.'

'I think you should tell him.'

'I know.'

I was clearly losing it. After the Baldwin beard confrontation I was starting to leak oil. My compass needle was spinning. I was contracting the disease that made me feel that maybe these guys knew better than me.

The police should have put me on producer's suspension.

A larger issue, and one that can profoundly haunt a production, is if a director starts shooting and then loses confidence in the script. This does not necessarily mean that the script is flawed. For months prior to the start date, Alfonso, Mitch, and I (and even Ethan) had worked on the script, making significant changes throughout. The hope is always that those early script concerns are worked out well ahead of time so that when the scenes are shot, they can be executed with confidence. Of course, rewrites are quite common during photography, but when they start to engulf the production, indecision and turmoil can result.

For those of you who have not seen the title page of a script after it has been filmed, ours looked like this:

GREAT EXPECTATIONS

screenplay by

Mitch Glazer

based on the novel

by

Charles Dickens

20th Century Fox
Producer - Art Linson
Director - Alfonso Cuaron

June 10, 1996
Blue Revision: June 20, 1996
Pink Revision: July 11, 1996
Green Revision: July 23, 1996
Yellow Revision: August 19, 1996
Goldenrod Revision: August 20, 1996
Salmon Revision: August 23, 1996
2nd Blue Revision: August 28, 1996
2nd Pink Revision: August 29, 1996
2nd Green Revision: September 9, 1996
2nd Yellow Revision: September 12, 1996
2nd Goldenrod Revision: Sept. 13, 1996
2nd Salmon Revision: September 16, 1996
3rd White Revision: September 24, 1996
3rd Blue Revision: September 27, 1996
3rd Pink Revision: October 1, 1996
3rd Green Revision: October 2, 1996
3rd Yellow Revision: October 4, 1996
3rd Goldenrod Revision: October 10, 1996

Notice the lower right corner. That is a list of revisions that took place, most of which occurred while we were shooting. There were many more rewrites, but these were the ones that made it into the script. If you examine the page closely, you see that the reworked pages of each revision were printed on a different color. I especially liked the salmon-colored pages. By the time De Niro was shooting his death scene, there were so many changes that the spine of the script looked psychedelic. From a producing standpoint, the impact of this can be immense. Naturally, with this much reexamination going on, a lot of disagreements emerge between the director and the writer. The producer, who also has a minor vote in all of this, helps to negotiate these issues. All of this occurs while the movie company is straining to get the day's work done and the actors are pleading for new pages so they can prepare.

Producers tend to approach this problem in different ways. I prefer to keep going with the writer that I started with, using that popular sports theory that it is best to stay with the player who got you there. In this case, Glazer's script got us to the starting gate. Other producers and directors prefer to use multiple writers, hoping to bring in different points of view. It is not uncommon for a movie to have exhausted ten writers and more to complete the job.

Often, the director doesn't even want the original writer around. His mere presence on the set becomes a distraction. When this happens, the neglected writer is either sequestered in a small section of a trailer trying to knock off pages, or he's left huddling by the crafts service truck eating doughnuts and making friends with grips and assorted workers from electrical.

On the other hand, some screenwriters simply refuse to visit a set. They can smell the impending ostracism. When we were doing *The Untouchables*, De Palma and I needed additional work from Mamet. I hoped to lure him by inviting him to Chicago. My thinking, of course, was that once David saw Sean Connery, Kevin Costner, and

De Niro, the enthusiasm of the crew and the beautiful production designs, he would get juiced up and jump in with some new pages. No chance. If I remember correctly, his response was something simple. Something like 'No.' When I suggested that he might have some fun dropping by, no writing required, it was as if the phone went dead. The silence continued until I said, 'Okay, I think I know how you feel about this.' I personally believe if you are trying to make a movie of substance, singularity of voice leads to the best results. When things are working correctly, the writer can give a movie as much cohesiveness as the director, and they both benefit from their collaboration.

It seems like several hundred years since Cameron Crowe wrote and Amy Heckerling directed *Fast Times at Ridgemont High*. Perhaps because of a dimming memory that's receding like a flushed toilet, or maybe because of the lingering ill effects from too many bad substances, I recall the making of that movie as a sunny and fresh experience. It was Cameron's first screenplay and it was Amy's first shot at directing a feature movie. They were wide-eyed, and so was I. In fact, it was so early on in my career that I still wanted to be a producer whom others could lean on.

Once Cameron finished the first draft, it was patently evident that his take on teen life in high school was authentic. He had spent a year infiltrating his high school and was able to mainline the source of his characters. Mind you, the studio was slightly horrified by the explicitness of the material, but the costs were so low that we were able to fly under the line of fire. Even though Amy, who was also a budding writer, wanted changes and adjustments to the script, Cameron had to be the guy who was going to see it through. He became a fixture on the set. As a result, many classic moments were created *after* filming began.

For those who want examples, three weeks into the shooting of *Fast Times*, when even the most nearsighted of executives were noticing that Sean Penn was stealing the movie, I did what any producer who was still breathing would do: I asked for more Spicoli scenes. Cameron, who was trailing the action and at our disposal at all times, came up with a few sequences, all of which ended up in the final cut. My favorite was a flashback with sportscaster Stu Nahan interviewing Jeff Spicoli after Spicoli had dreamed that he won the Hawaiian surfing championship. In the scene, Spicoli, buzzed on THC, clad in surfing shorts and Hawaiian leis and sandwiched between two perfect southern-California girls, is holding an oversize surf trophy. It was originally written for Spicoli to be a guest on the *Merv Griffin Show*, but Merv refused the part because of the drug references. When Nahan was the 'best' that we could get, Cameron readjusted the scene to accommodate the moment.

STU NAHAN
You know a lot of people expected Mark 'Cutback'
Davis or Bob 'Jungle' Gerard would take the honors this year.

JEFF SPICOLI
Those guys are FAGS!!!

STU NAHAN
That's fantastic . . . Let me ask you a question . . .
When you get out there, do you ever fear for your life?

JEFF SPICOLI
Well, Stu, I'll tell you, surfing is not a sport, it's a way of life . . . no hobby . . . it's a way of looking at that wave and saying, 'HEY, BUD, LET'S PARTY!'

Staying with the screenwriter who got you there has its rewards.
When things got hairy on *Great Expectations*, rightly or wrongly, I

was committed that Mitch should stay the course. I advised Alfonso that if he wanted changes, he should work with Mitch until he was satisfied. This process started early during preproduction and continued through filming. Somewhere in the centrifugal force of the collaboration, signs of differences were starting to surface. It wasn't that the screenplay wasn't working or that Alfonso's choices were wrong, it was that there seemed to be, at the core, a tonal difference among all of us in the way the movie was to be expressed. To put it simply, we were rarely on the same page.

The first hint that the differences were more than subtle occurred at the beginning of the schedule when we were shooting the scene of Finn, as a ten-year-old, when he falls hard for the ice princess Estella. The scene was originally filled with ten-year-olds' banter. Some good, some awkward. Alfonso replaced the scene with swirling tracking shots. In his attempt to make their first encounter more magical, he left out the dialogue completely, which he felt, I assumed, pulled against the intensity of the moment.

The situation became clear. Mitch's take was more comical and conversational; Alfonso's version was more visual and romantically seductive. A collision was inevitable. As we delved further into the film, Alfonso increasingly went for the visual moments. He either avoided the dialogue or kept insisting that Mitch rewrite much of it. What was interesting as the producer (the mayo) in this situation was that I had no particular point of view on who had the better approach. Mitch, being a close personal friend of mine, was encouraged by me, implored by me, to stay in the trenches. Which he did. I felt we had to try to accommodate Alfonso. The director, after all, is the final eye between the performance and what ends up on film. Hell, he *must* be accommodated. We were deep in the middle of shooting a movie. The alternative would be to get another writer, a move I was loath to make. To stay the course was to put two cats in a small paper bag.

With the pressure of the schedule and the ever-present fear that we might be making a heaping pile of garbage, the director gets openly temperamental. And so does everyone else. When things were going swell, Alfonso was charming and gracious. When things got ugly, he lurched out and blamed the script, the cast, and of course, the producer. It got so fucking weird that Alfonso, as time went on, would demand more and more pages and Mitch would keep writing. Mitch would bring pages to the set, and Alfonso, reading them in his director's chair, would let the pages fall slowly to the ground, one at a time, to show his displeasure. Mitch looked at me with that baleful expression 'I got married at your house, asshole . . . do something!' I looked back nonplussed, thinking, 'Who do I have to fuck to get off this set?' This did not augur well for ongoing working relationships. Mitch was disappointed with me for not completely supporting his effort, which is another way of saying 'This director is destroying my script.' Alfonso was disappointed with me for not helping him get the script exactly as he wanted it or enough money to make the masterpiece he was carrying around in his head. The studio was disappointed with me because we were over schedule and over budget, and I was disappointed that I ever got in the middle of this in the first place.

De Niro, as you might have assumed, enjoyed the experience immensely. He did end up, however, working more than seven days. I believe it was closer to twelve days, but this was hardly burdensome. He showed up at the beginning of the schedule in Florida, surprising us all with a shaved head, and went on to portray the escaped convict with his customary precision. Months later, at the very end of the schedule, he returned to the set for his death scenes. Unwittingly, he missed the agonizing middle.

By the time we were shooting nights in downtown Manhattan, everybody's nerves, except for his, were on red alert. De Niro's painstaking preparation for this sequence of scenes was taking several hours—something we had not taken into account when we planned the schedule. The crew was already in their final death dance. This phenomenon happens to all crews as a movie winds down. Their concentration already deadened and their eyes sunken from the ennui, they had begun their incessant chatter with each other about their next job, stopping only when Cuarón or I would brush past them on our way to the set. If the company were shooting in a swamp, we might have moved faster.

Bob was almost finished with his makeup when I entered his trailer. His long, gray-haired wig was in place, but only half of his full beard was stuck on. With the exposed padding around his waist, which was added to give him age, the overall look was almost clownlike. I had been pacing for the last half hour hoping my presence would speed things up. Ilona, De Niro's makeup artist extraordinaire, was slowly fussing with his beard. Out of frustration, I wanted to grab the glue and stick the fucker on myself. She looked at me warm and calm as if to say, 'Isn't making movies fun?' As I tried to tell Bob of all the pressure I'd been subjected to, how horrible the life of a producer was, he looked at me quizzically. I wasn't sure he was actually listening. I felt like Al Jolson on bended knee about to sing 'Mammy.'

'No more time, babe,' I said, looking at his reflection in the makeup mirror. 'We got no more time.'

'That's why you're great,' he said.

'Bob, you don't get it.'

'Do you want Ilona to make you something to eat?'

'No.'

'You sure?'

'We scheduled this scene of yours in two days . . . and the way we're goin' . . .'

'That's why you're great.'

'I need this one, Bob.'

'That's why you're great. I tell everyone.'

He smiled. He knew. It was going to be over when it was going to be over. We ended up losing another three days. The studio was freaked. Rothman even showed up on the set. He was wearing a baseball hat backward, but to no avail. The crew kept whispering, 'There's the suit, there's the suit.' By this time Rothman knew it was too late to salvage the schedule; he was just hoping to get an introduction to Gwyneth Paltrow.

De Niro, of course, impervious to it all, died with grace and style as a bum on a New York subway car and was paid like a king.

Throughout, the dailies looked excellent, but the internal chaos had had a broader effect, one not easily detected during filming. When the editing of the picture was completed, some holes remained in the story. I still don't know if it was because of undetected glitches in Glazer's script or because of Cuarón's ceaseless reworking of the script, but the connective tissue that linked the story was sorely lost. It became apparent that we would have to supply narration to smooth the transitions and to provide a Dickensian shading to the final cut. Again, I encouraged Mitch and Alfonso to take a crack at it and see if they could work together. Once the pressures of filming had ceased, Alfonso had considerably mellowed, but the damage was done. Putting Mitch and him in the same room was just too sweaty. Even though they attempted to lick it, Mitch, understandably, didn't have the heart for it and the effort was compromised.

I called David Mamet.

'What are you doing?' I asked.

'Nothin'.'

'Good. I got an idea.'

'Uh-huh.'

'I need your help.'

'Like a charity thing.'

'Not quite.'

'This help, do I get paid for it, or does 'help' mean I don't get paid?'

'The latter.'

'Oh.'

'Well, maybe I can get you a little money.'

'Okay, what is it?'

'D'you remember me telling you I'm producing *Great X*?'

'Yes, that's why you couldn't be in Canada the whole time looking after our bear movie.'

'That's right.'

'Well?'

'I need you to write some narration.'

'Oh, God.'

'The thing is crying for help.'

'Oh, no.'

'Consider it a favor.'

'Send it to me.'

'I already did, you'll have a tape of it tomorrow.'

'Okay.'

'Dave . . . I need this one.'

'If I do this . . . if I do this . . . hear me, I don't want *anyone* to know.'

'You have my word.'

All right. Here's a bit of the narration that opened the picture. The last line seems to have a prophetic resonance.

There either is or is not a Way Things Are. The color of the day, the way it felt to be a child, the feeling of salt water on your sunburned legs.

Sometimes the water is yellow and sometimes it is red.

But what color it may be in memory depends upon that day.

I'm not going to tell the story the way it happened. I'm going to tell it the way I remember it.

With Alfonso's lavish direction, Mitch's inventive screenplay, and spiked with Mamet's narration, we somehow wriggled our way to a decent picture. After this production wrapped, Mitch, Alfonso, and I didn't speak to each other for a couple of years. Some of the wounds are still wet.

TEN

PUSHING TIN DOWNHILL

The expression *pushing tin* is not an inside joke coined by a traveling tuna can salesman. In the dimly lit operations room of the New York Terminal Radar Approach Control, air traffic controllers say they are 'pushing tin' when referring to the daily grind of carefully guiding airplanes through the sky so they don't crash into each other. The allowable margin of error for this job is zero.

When I first read the article in the Sunday *New York Times Magazine*, written by Darcy Frey, documenting the horrors and the pressures of this occupation, my producer's heart started beating. The arena was a large room filled with radar scopes occupied by savagely bug-eyed air traffic controllers twitching and cursing as they tried to keep themselves from 'going down the pipes' – words used for the high anxiety of dealing with the possible near-miss or the midair collision that was always one bad mistake away. As the multitude of dots on their respective radar screens randomly run amok, reaching their peak on holiday weekends, the controller, to retain his sanity, has to convince himself that these little dots are not metal death ships filled with real people, they are just dots.

The maddening pressures inherent in the job are so extreme that all of these guys are emotionally kicked in the ass one way or another. They either drink, adopt weird physical tics, cheat on their wife, acquire peculiar superstitions, or just go categorically nuts. One guy, according to the article, while guiding ten jets in a great curving arc toward Newark, New Jersey, suddenly lost his communication system as he turned his pilots onto final approach. He rose from his chair shrieking and started tearing off his clothes. By the time someone stepped in to land the planes, he was quivering on the floor naked before being taken away. He was discharged on a medical leave until he could regain his wits. He tried a few times to visit his buddies at the TRACON station, but he never had the *cojónes* to return to the scopes again. When he did come in, his buddies looked the other way, superstitiously hoping that his bad juju wouldn't rub off on them.

What an arena! M.A.S.H. on wheels. The fallout of all this stress would be where the drama, the dark humor, and the morality tale would come together. There it was: The perfect setting for a movie. I figured it was so good, the geniuses at Fox would never get it.

I called Bill Mechanic and explained.

'Bill, we gotta buy this.'

'I agree.'

'But, Bill—'

'I agree.'

'Bill, it might be expensive.'

'I like it. Run it by Ziskin.'

I called Laura Ziskin, who was running Fox 2000.

'Laura, I just spoke to Bill.'

'I read the article.'

'Laura, we gotta get this.'

'I agree.'

Huh? This was eating ice cream for breakfast. Too easy. Within a week we were the proud owners of the article for the princely sum of $200,000, which included the right to use real moments from some of the controllers' lives. Things were so smooth, I started to hum the title song from *Car Wash*. I couldn't get the rhythm riff out of my head for three days. This must be what it's like to be Spielberg when he gets an itch for an idea. Everyone nods 'yes' like a spring-loaded doll's head. Didn't anybody stand up and ask, 'Who wants to see a bunch of nuts freaking out in front of radar screens and then go home and fuck their neighbor's wife?'?

Quite frankly, no.

The next step in the producer's handbook after securing the rights to a stellar idea is to hire a screenwriter. The story seemed to be shaping up as a drama/comedy exposing the foibles of people whose jobs put them under massive anxiety. Actually, at the time, we didn't know whether it would be a comedy or a drama or maybe both, but the delineation of that didn't concern us. It was going to be a movie about people crashing, not necessarily planes crashing. I began the agonizingly endless procedure of reading screenplays from lists and lists of writers who might be right for this kind of an idea, someone who understood how to write comedy while drawing from real situations and real people. If you are looking for excellence, the list narrows quickly. Very high in this group were Les Charles and Glen Charles, the brother team that was the creative force behind the classic television series *Cheers*. I was being diligent. In fact, the more I thought about the Charleses, the more I thought they would be ideal. I was about to call Ziskin to make my case when the phone rang.

'Hi, it's Laauurra,' she purred, always seeming to be surprised by the sound of her name.

'Hello, Laura.'

'I got an idea for you.'

'Good.'

'Do you know who the Charles brothers are?'

'Well, yeah, I wa—'

'Their agent just called the studio and said they want to write the air traffic thing.'

'Laura, they called *us?*'

'Yeah, he said they want to write it bad.'

'Laura, I was about to ca—'

'I think we should hire them.'

'Uh . . . me too.'

I must have been in dreamland.

'Laura, aren't they very expensive?'

'So what?'

Could this producing thing get any easier?

I learned later that while we at Fox were trying to buy the article, the Charles brothers had read it, liked it, and tried to buy the piece privately. We got there first. They liked it so much, however, they decided to offer their writing services anyway. A deal was quickly struck.

Working with the Charles brothers was interesting. They came from TV. There's a weird line drawn in Hollywood between those who work for television and those who work for movies. Granted, the line has been blurred on numerous occasions, but the way I see it, in most cases TV producers/writers end up with the money (real big money) and film people are mainly left with attitude. The earnings from the syndication rights from a hit television series are so vast that the recipients never have to work again. Glen and Les Charles never had to work again. This was new for me, working with screenwriters who are laced with money and have no attitude. They were even politically connected. During the prep period when our production staff was struggling to get access to some California TRACON facility, one of the brothers unassumingly said, 'Why don't I call Barbara Boxer [then a California U.S. senator]. I'm sure she or her office would be glad to help.' My God, a screenwriter with pull was almost an oxymoron.

Not only were they eager to write the script, they actually wanted to please us. They were always open to ideas, willing to collaborate, and available at all times to meet and rethink the direction we were going. Dealing with the Charles brothers was like melting butter. During filming, when I offered to fly them to the set in Toronto to discuss some additional script work, they politely declined our reimbursement gesture, saying they would come at their own expense. We soon discovered they had their own private plane and didn't want us to know they didn't like to fly commercial. It gets better. When the script was finally completed several months later, it was excellent.

It was just a first draft, but I decided to turn it in.

'Bill, what'ya think?'

'It's good.'

'Bill, is it too soon discuss the next step?'

'Go get a director.'

'Bill, that's the step I meant.'

'I know.'

Hmmmm.

'Hi, it's Laauurra.'

'What'ya think?'

'I really like it.'

'I'm so glad.'

'Go get me a list of directors.'

'Why not?'

It was *Groundhog Day* for producers. I woke up and everyone said 'yes.' I woke up the next day and everyone said 'yes' again. Hell, let's find a director.

Before I had a chance to really examine all of the possibilities, I got another call from Ziskin.

'Hi, it's Laauurra.'

'Hello, Laura.'

'What do you think of Mike?'

'Nichols?'

'No, Newell.'

'Oh.'

Mike Newell's star had been rising quickly. He had directed the low-budget comedy hit *Four Weddings and a Funeral* and the recently released *Donnie Brasco* with Al Pacino and Johnny Depp. Without my knowing him, he seemed to have the right sensibilities for this piece. Maybe I should think it over. Whom was I fooling? I thought he would be terrific. I just wished that I had thought of it.

'Well . . .,' I said.

'He's a friend of mine and I just talked to him about it,' she cooed.

'You did?'

'Guess what?'

'What?'

'He *responded*.'

'Is there anything I need to do?'

'Not really, I'll send it to him.'

'Okay, then.'

You get where this is going. Of course, Newell wanted to direct the movie. I became immobilized. I sat at my desk waiting for the phone to ring so I could yell, 'Blackjack!'

With Newell's commitment we were able to assemble an outstanding cast of special actors. John Cusack would play the high-flying air traffic controller Nick Falzone, the best of the best. That is, until the crazed daredevil Russell Bell, played by Billy Bob Thornton, comes to town and derails him. As they engage in games of one-upmanship, their respective wives, Cate Blanchett and Angelina Jolie, get embroiled in the complicated mess.

To save money we agreed to shoot the movie in Toronto and make it look like Long Island. Production went along swimmingly. The dailies looked good. In one scene, Angelina Jolie grabs Billy Bob's ass, then nuzzles his neck, which made me think that was some damn fine acting until I was told they had fallen in love on the set for real. We even stayed on budget and pretty much kept to the schedule. We all got along, and even the artistic disagreements were manageable. But by now, you already knew that.

There was only a minor hint that everything might not be kismet. After the movie was screened in Los Angeles, I was walking down the hallway by the marketing division, near Bob Harper's office, where I thought I overheard a female voice saying, 'Does anyone really want to see John Cusack naked?' I stopped to listen for the answer. I leaned into the doorway. Too late. Two secretaries looked up. The moment had passed, and I chose to ignore it. Anyway it was compensated for by Peter Travers's *Rolling Stone* review, which said, 'Like the best movies, *Pushing Tin* takes us into a new world. And this world, which finds fresh hell in the phrase "fear of flying," is a *lulu*. It's rowdy, raunchy, and action-packed, even if it is bound to turn audiences into infrequent fliers.'

A couple of weeks after *The Matrix* overwhelmed the box office, our movie opened in eighteen hundred theaters, April 23, 1999.

Total cost: $38,000,000.

Total domestic gross: $8,400,000.

Do the math.

ELEVEN

THE FOX AND THE HOUND

'Get it, Jerry . . . *do the math*.'

'I get it.'

'You see what I'm sayin'?'

'Sure, sure.'

'Stay with me, Jerry.'

'I am. I liked the last bit.'

Greased on wine and waiting for dessert, Jerry had conspicuously lost interest in my journey. By this time, Giorgio's was packed. Getting from one table to the next required moving and bumping into people's seats just to get to the door. Each table was filled with some Hollywood type. Agents, producers, writers, directors, and those that service these people were all jammed together. Oddly, even though all the patrons knew that the layout of the room forced intimacy, each person was doing his best to ignore the others. Jerry was completely moonstruck. His mood had turned wistful and sour simultaneously. He was no longer paying much attention to what I had to say.

'Look who's here.'

'Jerry, look who isn't here.'

'No, turn your head to the right over that fat girl in leather pants.'

'I don't turn.'

'It's Ovitz.'

'Uh-huh.'

'Well, it's interesting's all.'

'What's interesting about it, Jerry?'

'He's gritty, I'll give him that.'

'A real battering ram,' I said.

'What a shame, huh?'

'What part?'

'Falling off the power chart'n' all.'

'Shit happens quick.'

'It's cyclical, don't you think?'

'Like a karma thing, Jerry?'

'That's right.'

'I see . . . what comes around . . .'

'Yeah, it's a circle, pal. Ovitz shoved some testicles down some people's throats and then, of course, Eisner shoved them down his throat.'

'Not exactly.'

'Well, he did get a ninety-million-dollar check as a booby prize.'

'Jerry, I'm glad to see you keep current.'

'You gotta like it, it's got symmetry.'

At that moment, Ovitz and his group got up to leave. They had to make the uncomfortable slide past our table. He got so close, I had to move my chair forward. As he tapped my shoulder to get through, I was forced to turn. He glared down on us, semisurprised, with a steeled grin. The effort made him appear as if his dinner had suddenly rotted from the inside. My first reaction was to say, 'It's not my fault,' but I went the other way.

'Hey, Mike. You, of course, know Jerry.'

Ovitz glanced at Jerry, then looked for another escape route, but he was trapped.

'Before you did,' he said through his teeth.

'Hiya, Mike.'

'Hello, Jerry.'

I pushed my chair off to the left, giving Mike a bit more space to get through. He darted off.

'Great to see you,' I said.

'Yeah,' he said.

That was it, short and uncomfortable. I looked over at Jerry. I could only imagine what sort of horror had occurred between those two when Jerry was still in action. Both were well known for inflicting pain, a great deal of pain, when they enjoyed the upper hand. We sat there in silence until Ovitz finally made it through the door.

'Let me tell you a story.'

'Go ahead, Jerry, I'm a sucker for showbiz stories.'

'No. It's a World War Two story, s'got nothing to do with Tinsel Town.'

'Go for it.'

'It was during the final stages of the war. Himmler was the head of the Gestapo. You remember Himmler, right?'

I nodded.

'Sometime in the early part of 1944, he was hosting an awards dinner for his men. They had just finished a sumptuous meal, had drunk cases of the finest French Bordeaux *rouge*, when Himmler proudly got up to make a toast, celebrating their effort in the final solution. Standing in front of a giant swastika, he removed his side pistol and clanged it against his glass, calling for quiet. "Gentlemen," he went on to say, "in the future, our future, history will record that one of our greatest accomplishments. . . ." Himmler took a pause for emphasis. "We did the thing we had to do while never losing our innate sense of *decency*." '

Jerry then fell silent. I dug deep trying to respond. I even opened my mouth a couple of times, but nothing surfaced.

I called for the check.

TWELVE

FIGHT CLUBBED

The exterior door to Screening Room C opened abruptly and out spilled seven of nine Fox film executives. Two of them remained inside. It was late in the afternoon on the Fox lot, and the deep shadows from the surrounding buildings camouflaged their expressions as they tried to adjust their eyes to the daylight. The director, David Fincher, and I had just screened a high-quality video rough cut of *Fight Club*. At one time or another over the past eighteen months, this group had all read some incarnation of the script, and a few of them had even watched some of the dailies. This was the day that they experienced the full impact of what they had paid for. The anticipation had been high. After all, the movie starred Brad Pitt, Edward Norton, and Helena Bonham Carter and was directed by one of the truly gifted young filmmakers. The last time Fincher and Pitt had joined forces, the movie *Se7en* had surprised everyone in Hollywood with its riveting originality and, more important, its over three-hundred-million-dollar worldwide grosses.

Numbers like that can make an executive's year. Hell, in most cases, that kind of success can define his or her tenure. The executives might not have admitted it, but they had as much personally riding on the outcome of *Fight Club* as did the film-makers. They walked in, almost giddy, all smiles and chatty, backslapping and hugging Fincher before taking their seats. The mere possibility that Fincher and Pitt might provide the same kind of lightning a second time made them all rubbery with expectation.

I had met David five years earlier when he was editing *Alien 3*. I'm not sure how the meeting came about, but I received a call that he was interested in talking to me about some ideas. I'd heard that he'd had a difficult time dealing with the studio on his first movie, so I assumed he was interested in taking advantage of a producing partner on future stuff. He was already being touted as a wunderkind. He had a big rep as a sophisticated music-video director, had done some remarkable commercials, had dated Madonna, and although he was still in his twenties, Fox (under the Joe Roth regime) had given him one of their family jewels, an *Alien* sequel, to be his first feature directing assignment.

He was unassuming. His office was bare: two chairs and an empty desk. He told me that he used to work as a projectionist in Oregon and had seen hundreds of movies, even some forgettable movies that I was involved in, hundreds of times.

'I'm working on something that interests me.'

'I'd love to hear it.'

'Let me tell you the opening.'

'Great.'

'Manhattan's Lower East Side is crisscrossed with magnetic lines for elevated trains. These magnetic tracks cut massive chunks through the old buildings to make room for the high-speed cornering of the train cars.'

'Nice.'

'Three guys enter a Lower East Side Manhattan hovel carrying pizza and begin to watch television. Inside the kitchen, we see a figure dressed in a full-length coat and glacier glasses hanging upside down outside the window. One of the guys enters to get a beer. Suddenly the guy with the glasses is standing next to him by the refrigerator. He shoots him with a dart gun in the throat, walks into the TV room, announces that he is body hunter number 209, says, "All of your rights are rescinded," and coldly shoots the rest of them in the throat.'

'Okay.'

'He then proceeds to take out large plastic sheets, spread them on the floor, and line up the bodies in a symmetrical row. He thoughtfully closes their eyes, inserts a large rubber plug in his mouth, and begins to smear his face with thick Vaseline. The rubber plug serves as an air hole. He then takes out a laser knife and splits each body from the esophagus to the pubic bones, rips them apart, and methodically removes the kidneys and other assorted organs.'

'I see.'

'He carefully places each organ in separate plastic bags, and leaves.'

'So, who's going to get this guy?'

'No one.'

'He gets away with it?'

'No. No. *He's* our *hero*.'

'The guy with the plastic bags filled with organs?'

'Yeah. What do you think?'

This was vintage Fincher taking delight in the wild mixture of irreverence and audaciousness. His first movie had yet to be released and he was already excited about ideas that were almost indefensible in the corporate culture that would pay for it. At the time, we were still climbing out of the Reagan years, with a climate in Hollywood that made making this kind of movie almost unthinkable. In addition, I was at the point in my life where coasting downhill had enormous appeal. This guy was trouble. I knew I was around somebody whose ambition was to maul and excite. I wasn't sure I had the stomach anymore for the fight. I liked him, but I could barely muster the energy to say, 'Very nice to meet you, I've gotta go.'

The screening of *Fight Club* was about to start. I moved to a seat near the door. Then, after the lights went down, I spent most of my time standing in the back of the room. I found that whenever I was at an early screening, I got too caught up in watching those who were watching, and I completely lost my concentration for the film. I couldn't help it. So as not to distract the person next to me, I preferred to observe the audience from the rear. In this case, the studio's reaction turned out to be a hard read.

A costly title sequence filled the screen. With the music blasting, a computer-generated tracking shot pierces the darkness and flies through the motor neurons, navigating the folds of a human brain, revealing electron-microscopic synapses squirting clouds of cerebral fluid, for some ninety seconds, until it emerges from the prefrontal lobe above the eyes to reveal a badly beaten Edward Norton. And then the shot pulls farther back to reveal a loaded .38 jammed into his face.

This was a quick appetizer from the mind and imagination of the hot chef in town. Fincher had devised this intro with Digital Domain before he'd ever started to shoot *Fight Club*, but permission to execute it was only granted later by the studio as a sugar bonus for his being *good* – a euphemism for his keeping on schedule. I glanced around the screening room. They were hooked.

When the unnamed narrator, whom we call Jack (Edward Norton), was smothered by the huge breasts of a large fat man (Meat Loaf) while participating in a support group for those suffering from testicular cancer, the executives were so still you could watch the movie reflected off their eyeglasses. I remember that Ziskin, who had left us pretty much alone during the start of filming, was concerned about the giant nipples on the giant breasts and wanted them removed from the fat suit, or at least not have them appear so erect. Fincher denied the request; the nipples remained vast and hard.

Moments later, when Marla enters the hall (Helena Bonham Carter's introduction), chain-smoking, and interrupts the all-male testicular support group with the line 'This is cancer, right?' the executives froze. Did we go too far? A woman in sunglasses joining a testicular cancer meeting! Every time I've watched this scene, I've laughed. But there were no chuckles from this group. For the remainder of the first hour, they sat absolutely motionless, as if they were marines on full parade. No hand movements, no facial spasms, nothing. They were either rapt or stunned or both.

In the second hour, I began to notice that some of the women, and a couple of the men, would occasionally jerk their heads backward, a sudden ticlike movement, as if they were trying to avoid a collision. When Tyler (Brad Pitt), in front of his men, begged his assailant (Lou) to hit him again even harder, even though his face was already pulverized, a young assistant to Ziskin put her hands over her eyes and dropped her head. I was getting apprehensive, but I could tell they were jolted.

Perhaps one of the most provocative scenes in the movie is where Tyler initiates Jack into the mayhem with a savage acid/lye burn to the hand in the form of a kiss. While Jack is overwhelmed by the searing pain and quivers around the room in tears, Tyler, the darkly drawn devil in all of us, grabs him by the arm. Jack tries to pull his hand free. Tyler won't let go. Jack tries to think of a series of images to distract himself from the overwhelming pain. Tyler doggedly insists Jack confront the moment while he explains its purpose:

TYLER
This is the greatest moment of your life and you're off somewhere, missing it.

JACK
No, I'm not . . .

TYLER
Shut up. Our fathers were models for God.
And, if our fathers bailed, what does that tell us about God?

JACK
I don't know . . .

Tyler SLAPS Jack's face again.

TYLER
Listen to me. You have to consider the possibility that God doesn't like you, he never wanted you. In all probability, he hates you. This is not the worst thing that can happen . . .

JACK
It isn't . . . ?

TYLER
We don't need Him . . .

JACK
We don't . . . ?

TYLER
Fuck damnation. Fuck redemption. We are God's unwanted children, and so be it . . .

Jack looks at Tyler – they lock eyes. Jack does his best to stifle his spasms of pain. He bolts toward the sink, but Tyler holds on.

TYLER
You can run water over your hand or use vinegar to neutralize the

burn, but first you have to give up. First you have to know, not fear, that someday, you are going to die. Until you know that and embrace that, you are useless.

JACK

You . . . you don't know what this feels like, Tyler.

Tyler shows Jack a LYE-BURNED KISS SCAR on his own hand.

TYLER

It's only after you've lost everything that you're free to do anything.

Tyler grabs a bottle of VINEGAR – pours it over Jack's wound. Jack slumps to the floor.

There are tears in Tyler's eyes.

TYLER

Congratulations. You're a step closer to hitting bottom.

There was no need to check out the audience anymore. Instead, I glanced over at Fincher. He was curiously relaxed. He looked like a man who was getting his money's worth. He wasn't at all concerned if the impact of what he had done was gratifying to them or not. He knew he was doing something to these onlookers, something darkly powerful, and that pleased him.

One of the true surprises for me during the making of *Fight Club* was Brad Pitt. He never showed any evidence of an actor who was out there trying to protect his 'Brad Pitt–ness.' Usually when this happens to a young actor, the first instinct is hang on and play it safe.

He doesn't want to fuck things up. And for sure, his manager, agent, and lawyer don't want to fuck things up. An awful lot of money is at stake. The result is that actors tend to repeat the same performances and the same kind of roles that created the most success. Without a shred of false vanity or the use of old tricks to win over an audience, Pitt proved to be a formidable actor of enormous talent. Can anyone imagine, thirty years ago, Robert Redford or Warren Beatty shaving his head or working without caps on his teeth or exposing himself so raw and ruthless as Brad had done and just let the chips fall? With all the hype that's associated with movie stardom, I was not expecting Brad to be almost reckless about challenging the boundaries of what others were expecting him to do. His work in *Fight Club* was stellar.

Five minutes were left before the movie ended. On the screen, Jack had just blown a hole through Tyler's head. I headed for the door. Soon Marla would join Jack on the top floor of an unoccupied office building to witness the total annihilation of a simulated Century City from a series of bombs that were planted by Project Mayhem. A massive explosion would rattle the glass walls as buildings collapsed into each other and imploded in a cloud of dust. Jack, utterly beaten and bloodied, would wearily turn to Marla and end with the ironic line 'I'm sorry . . . you met me at a very strange time in my life.'

I positioned myself around the corner of the theater, trying to get a candid bead on the results. Remember, even if a picture 'falls off the screen,' key executives must go over and congratulate the director. Also, *Fight Club* had yet to be tested on a preview audience, so no matter what these executives actually thought of the movie on their own, the preview audience would eventually redefine those feelings. Even if they were apprehensive, it was too soon for them to overreact. Should the audience response turn out to be grand, they wouldn't want to be remembered as naysayers.

Robert Harper, the marketing executive, was the first to exit.

'Hey, how 'bout that, huh?' I asked.

He looked pissed off, annoyed that I was already waiting for him. He nodded silently in my direction without facing me. He put on his sunglasses and walked stiffly back to the administration building. That he didn't stay to commiserate with Bill Mechanic or the other executives could mean several things. He was just a marketing guy. It was too soon to draw any conclusions.

Tom Sherak, in his fifties, was then a high-ranking executive at Fox, theoretically in charge of distribution. This meant he was responsible for strategizing when and how many theaters a movie was to be released in, as well as for negotiating the specific terms with the theater owners. He reported to Mechanic, who reported to Chernin, but Sherak had been at Fox for twenty-five years, long before they were ever there. He knew where all of the skeletons were hidden, and he was smart enough to avoid involving himself in the content of a picture. It wouldn't have mattered anyway because the executives above him, who thought of themselves as creative types, weren't too concerned with his artistic opinions. In truth, they didn't really give a shit. Tom was the guy that booked the movies into theaters. If they were bad, he could always blame the other Fox managers, who prided themselves on being a whole lot hipper than Sherak.

Through the years, I felt that Tom, a truly decent guy, would reflect the barometric pressure of the theater owners but not necessarily the audience. So when I saw him step out from the screening room, I was curious. It might have been my twisted imagination, but he seemed slightly disoriented. He shuffled around the parking lot like a man behind a couple of stiff margaritas struggling to remember where he had parked his car. I guessed the movie had gotten to him.

'Hey, Tom.'

'Whoa, whoa.' He held his hand up as a shield.

'Tom, I know it's probably not your thing but . . .'

'What *is* it?'

I began walking with him toward the administration building. 'Tom, it's a terrific movie is what it is.'

He looked at me queerly, trying to gauge my sincerity. He started to walk faster. 'Well, there's a lot going on, I'll give you that.'

'It's about the disillusionment of an entire young male generation.'

'Huh?'

'You know feelings of emasculation, materialism run amok, *rage*.'

'Huh?' He shook his head. It seemed to me that he just wanted to go home and hug his family.

'Tom, you gotta admit it's funny.'

'No.'

'Yes.'

'No. Don't say that.'

'I'll grant you, I was surprised that nobody laughed, but this movie is *funny*.'

'I didn't see funny.'

'Trust me, it's funny.'

'I want you to do me a favor.'

'Sure, Tom.'

'Next week, I have a psychiatrist—'

'But, I . . .'

'I want you to pick a day, any day, and I would like you to go with me and explain this to him, in my presence, why you think this thing is *funny*.'

'Tom, do you really think that's necessary?'

'Absolutely.'

'I got a full week.'

'It would do you some good.'

'Thanks anyway.'

'I think I know funny,' he said.

Watching him walk away, I realized then that when the exhibitors saw the movie, they were going to freak. Incidentally, in Sherak's defense, when he did see *Fight Club* the second and third time, with a younger audience that understood and responded to the humor, he admitted that although he hadn't warmed to it the first time, the more he saw it, the funnier and better it became.

Mechanic and Ziskin finally emerged from the theater. They were white. They had thinly creased smiles etched on their faces, but it was evident to me that they weren't sure what had just happened and were even less sure what was going to happen. They had a lot of personal career dreams wrapped up in this high-profile movie. If they had guessed right, they would be lionized. If they had guessed wrong, who knows, they might just have to pack up their underwear and ignominiously face their futures as independent film producers. That sort of fate can drain the blood from the hardiest of executives.

Throughout the film's production, Mechanic – especially Mechanic – had taken on the pressure with a wavering composure. He had stood up for *Fight Club* as boldy as he could, but after this screening, he knew that if this baby didn't fly, there might be a huge career price to pay. Gearing up for this eventuality was obviously causing some wear and tear. His eyes were slightly dilated, his shoulders a bit more slumped. He looked like one of those good high-stakes poker players in Las Vegas who, having just had all of his fingers broken, and having lost his entire stake, wanly addresses the crowd, 'A mere flesh wound, ladies and gents, a mere flesh wound.'

Mechanic and Ziskin made their way over to Fincher to praise him. Ziskin clasped her palms together in prayer mode, touched her fingers to her mouth, spread her legs slightly for better balance, and almost knelt before him, saying, 'Gosh, David, you've really done it this time.' Then she continued with something along the lines of 'I've got some issues, of course, it's all in the details, you know . . . there's lots to talk about . . . but . . . what a, what a, what a . . .'

Mechanic gestured stiffly to me with his hand, then nodded at Fincher, as if to reassure himself that everything was going to be all right. I figured he was already privately rehearsing how to explain this time bomb to Murdoch and Chernin. This left him even more preoccupied. When he finally spoke to Fincher, he mustered something brave like 'Powerful, very powerful . . .' Fincher smiled back and graciously thanked him. Then Mechanic addressed me with one of those fateful lines: 'I don't care what anyone says, I'm proud of it, really, really proud of it.' Uh-oh.

What was clear was that nobody would be able to come up with a simple, concise response to this early cut that would calm their nerves and make the journey more palatable. I recall when Brian De Palma and I presented *The Untouchables* to the Paramount executives for the first time, they were concerned about the violence. The executives focused on the shoot-out at the train-station stairs, where 'the bookkeeper' gets shot in the head against a marble wall. As he slid down the wall, De Palma revealed remnants of his brain, hair, and blood sticking to the marble. The executives had convinced themselves that this was the singular moment in the movie destined to turn off women. They knew we were not going to touch the soon to be famous Capone/baseball-bat sequence. So, instead of giving us a laundry list of suggestions, it became easier for them to focus on this one incident and try to get us to tone it down.

At the customary meeting the next day, they made their case. De Palma considerately said, 'Okay, let me take a look at it.' When we walked out, I asked him what his intentions were, since both of us liked that shot. He turned to me and said, 'Two words: *final cut*.'

So many incidences in *Fight Club* were alarming, no group of executives could narrow them down. It's not as if, let's say, they could suggest cutting the scene with Chloe (the terribly disturbing Meryl Streep look-alike skeletal cancer victim who fancied Jack) and everything would be okay. I had felt the screening room collectively wince when Chloe talked about how she's learned to face death but all she really wants to do 'is get laid for the last time.' Or, if not that scene, perhaps they might suggest losing the sex scene between Marla and Tyler, where Brad, leering naked in the doorway, wearing a yellow rubber glove with Marla reeling from ecstasy in the background, asks Norton if he would like to 'finish her off.' Or, what about the scene where Tyler and Jack steal real human fat from a liposuction clinic to make designer soap and end up spilling it all over themselves while attempting to escape over a chain-link fence? Or, remember when Tyler, working as a movie projectionist, spliced a single frame of a man's penis into children's films? Or . . .

Mechanic and Ziskin had been through many tough screenings before, but this mélange was going to put them thoroughly to the test. Before any meaningful comments could be made, they badly needed to regroup. It was like spitting in a hurricane. I loved the movie. It was so audacious that it couldn't be brought under control. Soon Murdoch and Chernin would be flopping around like acid-crazed carp wondering how such a thing could even have happened.

Fincher was leaning against the outside wall of the screening room, waiting patiently for the executives to leave. The film's guerrilla assault was so potent that many viewers were initially going to get sidetracked from appreciating some of the ground-breaking techniques that were on display. But Fincher knew that. From a directing standpoint there were so many daring moments. The 'jiggled camera' scene where Tyler, glaring in the lens, was saying, 'You are not your job . . . you are not your khakis,' while the frame around him was coming apart as if self-destructing in the movie projector, was one of several innovative sequences that had never before been seen. Perhaps my favorite magic trick was Fincher's rendering of the psychological cat-and-mouse game that culminates with Jack realizing that the only way he can get rid of Tyler is to shoot himself in the mouth. Jack jams the barrel into his own mouth, pulls the trigger, and fires a bullet. The monster explosion lights up his jaw cavity, blows open his cheeks like Dizzy Gillespie's. The bullet rips through the side of his face, but he miraculously survives. It's so real you'd think Norton might have killed himself while trying to do the scene, and it's so seamless that if you go frame by frame on a DVD player, it still gets your attention.

In short, Fincher had made the movie he wanted to make. Its essence was frozen in concrete. If you could have pulled him aside and asked him what sort of relief he could offer any of these Fox guys, in the form of modifying the cut, he would have shrugged and said, as he had often said, 'There's nothing *to* do, we didn't make this movie for *them*.'

I wanted to suggest to Mechanic and Ziskin that they go get drunk or whistle in a graveyard. I thought better of it. It was time for the producer to be seen and not heard. There was nowhere else for them to go. Finally, they turned to Fincher and said something like, 'Terrific . . . uh, work . . . uh, uh . . . we'll talk tomorrow.'

We knew by now that when *Fight Club* hit the streets, at least the reaction wouldn't be lukewarm. The critics ran the gamut from 'bold, brilliant, and inventive' to 'loathsomely indefensible.' It became the kind of thing that if you loved it, truly loved it, you would be deeply suspicious of those who didn't connect with it. What I hadn't anticipated was the dramatic response from those who were uncomfortable with it. They almost wanted to punish those responsible for this 'heinous' act. I remember a couple of months after the picture was released, I ran into Robbie Friedman, a high-ranking executive at Paramount Pictures, and a friend of mine. All he could do was shake his head.

'How could you?' he asked.

'Huh?'

I was about to start with 'Don't blame us producers, we're just the monkeys that do the dishes,' or better yet, the more confrontational approach, 'You stupid bastard, it's a brilliant movie, and anyways, you must admit it's darkly funny,' but by that time I'd already been down that road too many times.

The movie opened to lackluster domestic box office results, largely due, I believe, to an ill-conceived one-dimensional Bob Harper marketing campaign. Wait. Is there a producer still breathing who doesn't blast the poor marketing stiff for his failed movies? It's Producing 101 to blame somebody else. Frankly, with all of the time I've spent in this town, I'd like to think I'm above all that, but I'm not.

That icy demeanor I spotted after Harper left the screening room that day turned out to be more than just cramps from his commissary lunch. Deep down, he didn't really like the movie, and many would say, 'Who can blame him?' Nonetheless, it's an awkward job to try to sell something that you either don't understand or don't really like. In his case he was too reluctant to admit he didn't understand the movie's intentions, fearing that he would expose himself as no longer au courant. Instead of abdicating the responsibility of the campaign to Fincher and other vendors who had a feel for their audience, he smugly kept control of it. The result was an initial campaign that only sold the titillation of young guys beating the shit out of each other without letting the audience know of the much smarter and wittier ironic purpose to the whole journey. It was a knuckleheaded move.

The first couple of weeks after we returned from the Venice Film Festival were edgy. Mechanic's early prediction was that the movie's losses would be substantial. The 'I told you so people' were temporarily buoyed until the foreign box office improved the number significantly, and then the DVD came out, with a new campaign, to become one of the largest-selling DVDs in Fox's history. In the end, Mechanic revised his estimate and said that the film would eventually return a small but definite ten-million-dollar profit. Of course, when Bill told me this at the Polo Lounge, eighteen months later, he was no longer working at Fox and neither was Laura Ziskin.

And neither was I.

After the screening, as Fincher and I watched Mechanic and Ziskin weave their way back to their respective offices, huddled in conversation, I swear I could hear Procol Harum's 'A Whiter Shade of Pale' come drifting over the soundstages.

THIRTEEN

SUNSET STRIPPED NAKED

Here's a bitter tale. This is where vanity and greed override any sane producing principles to such a degree that it's a wonder I talked myself through it. When you consider all the excellent ideas there are for a producer to draw from, when you think of all the great books and writers that he can buy or steal from to invent a movie, imagine what kind of hefty weirdness it took for me to try to carve a movie out of my own life experience, stuff that took place more than twenty-five years ago. And worse, sugarcoat it, just so I can get the fucker made. I realize that this outburst is vague and ill defined, but it's a place to start. I produced a movie called *Sunset Strip*. It was my last movie for Fox. I know the title doesn't ring a bell because the movie was released in one theater in Los Angeles, for only one weekend, before being trash-heaped into the discounted-video bins. There are worse things that can happen to a movie producer, but they usually involve a life-threatening illness to irreplaceable organs. As always, I went into this adventure with high hopes. But good wishes are never enough. In fact, I'd say they're not to be trusted. Working through this, perhaps we can both come to understand that golden rule of producing: 'Hand someone his lunch before he hands it to you.'

'Jerry, look at you, you're still happening.'

'Whad'ya mean?'

'Your car is already waiting for you.'

'As it should be.'

We were standing on the sidewalk outside Giorgio's, directly across the Pacific Coast Highway. You could hear the waves crashing on State Beach behind the volleyball courts. Jerry was getting weary. What had initially been a vicarious thrill, listening to my tales of woe mixed with gossip and failure, was starting to reverse itself. He had become more reticent. His vulgar references to dark body parts three months ago were slowly being replaced by sighs and far-off stares. I couldn't tell whether he was thinking about his withering digestion or whether he was scheming his reentry into the Hollywood fray.

The power to green-light movies leaves a tattooed imprint on the soul. That unquenchable urge to walk around town saying 'When *I made* that film' never goes away. Who could blame a deposed movie despot for claiming a bit of authorship? It was merely a petty theft. A misdemeanor. Think of it. You're a studio executive who just put a big hit movie into play (let's say *The Nutty Professor*) and you are surrounded by greedy well-wishers from the industry wondering how *you made* it. Is it not an irresistible urge to say, 'Thanks, fellas, but you should have seen the three-hour rough cut. Well, the damn thing fell off the screen. Woowee, it was hard sledding, but once I got in there, I really turned that bitch around.' Rarely is this conversation within earshot of the director or the screenwriter, and it is never heard by the film's editor because they never get invited within two blocks of a studio executive. Unfortunately, taking credit for other people's work is not limited to studio executives; producers share the disease as well.

Jerry would never admit it, but the more we talked about one asshole topping another asshole in Hollywood, the more his cravings to get back were awakened. Since he had once been considered one of the major assholes in Hollywood, a source of much personal pride, our little chats only reminded him that the word *major* had inexorably been deleted from his letterhead. I wasn't sure, but I felt he still wanted to kick some ass.

'Jerry, how 'bout that, the guy didn't even ask you for a ticket.'

'I didn't get a ticket.'

'But you never come here.'

'I know.'

'How did he remember?'

'I slipped him twenty bucks when I drove in.'

'But if you took a ticket, it would only cost you five dollars.'

'I know, that's the beauty of it: *no* ticket.'

'I don't get it.'

'No ticket.' He held up his palms like a Vegas croupier.

'You do see that it cost you an extra fift—'

'To avoid the indignity of holding a ticket.'

'Of course, what was I thinking?'

I was still drawing sustenance from these gatherings. More directly, I needed them.

'So, what'll it be for next week?' I asked.

'What'dya mean, like Chinese or sushi?'

'Well, yes.'

'I don't think so.'

'Jerry, you're kidding.'

'No.'

I needed Jerry; I had to boost his spirits.

'But I only got a little bit to go.'

'Can I be straight with you?'

'Why not?'

'You don't have enough power in the business to keep up my enthusiasms.'

'What about my movie that didn't get released?'

'Small potatoes, babe.'

'I need one more shot.'

'Lemme think about it.'

For twenty bucks the car attendant partially bowed when Jerry approached his car. Without acknowledging either of us, Jerry got in and drove off.

In the spring of 1969, in front of the Whisky A Go-Go, on the Sunset Strip, John Phillips, leader of the Mamas and the Papas, wearing a psychedelic robe and a Russian fur hat, slid out of a vintage Rolls-Royce creamed on acid. As he slipped past me with a generous smile, certain that the world was his playground, I tried to remind him that we had a meeting at Universal at ten o'clock in the morning. I was there because I was working for him. What's interesting from a movie-producing perspective was that in those days rock-and-roll royalty were the stars of the neighborhood. They had that heat the movie and television minions were chasing. On any night the cast of characters circling the Whisky was a microcosm of bizarre Hollywood hopefuls, from agents and publicists dressed in tie-dyed shirts and beads, to young Midwestern girls just off the bus looking for Jim Morrison. If you threw a party and John Lennon or Bob Dylan or Mick Jagger was going to show up, everyone clamored for an invitation. Actors wished they could play the guitar. For a brief time, movie stars were in second position.

At that time, I was employed by Phillips and his partner Lou Adler with the intention of helping them get a foothold in the movie industry. The vast success of the Mamas and the Papas was fading, and they were looking for new conquests. They had already been toying with 'movie ideas' and they needed someone to get them in the door. I think I was chosen for the task because I was cheap. Their most recent idea was a twist on Mary Shelley's life with Byron, which John Phillips wanted to write with Michael Sarne *(Myra Breckinridge)* for Sarne to direct. My job was to get a studio to listen. I was so fresh at the movie game that even though I was aware of the key

Hollywood players, it was still a struggle to get any of them on the phone. I had to fake it.

At MCA/Universal there was a young, square-jawed executive, Ned Tanen, who was put in charge of the movie division. Prior to his promotion, I knew that he had had substantial success in the music business. I figured he would be the obvious choice to have an affinity for these guys. That's all I knew. I did not know how to get an introduction to him, and I could hardly admit to my employers that I needed their help to set up a meeting. I tried for several days to reach Tanen on the phone, but to no avail. Finally, I resorted to that terrible Hollywood device of telling his secretary it was someone else calling.

'Would you tell Mr. Tanen that Lou Adler is calling?' I asked.

'Please hold.'

'Sure thing.'

Adler was a highly visible and successful record producer. He reverberated style from the sixties and seventies. Bearded and known for wearing odd caps and shoes, he was the kind of guy whom I thought Tanen would be eager to be in business with.

'Can I have Mr. Adler's number? Mr. Tanen will have to call back.'

Well, that was the last hope. Five minutes later the phone rang.

'Hello, Adler residence,' I said in a slightly altered voice. We were working out of Adler's house across the street from the Bel Air Hotel.

'Mr. Tanen returning.'

'Lou'll be right there,' I said in an even higher voice.

Click.

'Hello.'

'Lou?'

'Ned?'

'Lou?'

'Not really. I'm really sorry. I'm not Lou. I work for Lou and I'm trying to get you to meet with him and John Phillips to discuss a movie idea.'

Complete silence.

I don't recommend children trying this at home. After a brief awkward pause, I couldn't tell whether Tanen had put me on hold without responding or had done the right thing and hung up on me. Just as I was about to drop the phone, his secretary returned and said that he would be willing to schedule a meeting the following Wednesday at ten in the morning. I thanked her. I had broken through. John and Lou had their movie meeting with the head of Universal Pictures, and they had assumed that I'd done it with aplomb.

By the time I had picked up Lou and driven up to 783 Bel Air Road to John Phillips's house, it was 9:30 A.M. This still gave us an ample half hour to drive over the hill to Universal Pictures and get there on time. The home looked deserted as we drove up the long driveway; the only thing that seemed to be moving were a couple of plumed peacocks. They were roaming across the front lawn between four Rolls-Royces haphazardly parked near the entrance. It was a large Tudor-style home perched on a Bel Air hill overlooking the ocean. What had once been occupied by Jeanette MacDonald was now home to rockers wanting to smother themselves in grandeur.

The front door and the two side windows were wide open, but the house seemed to be unoccupied. Adler and I got out of the car and entered the foyer. In an alcove off to the left, on a gray slate floor, was an empty baby casket converted into a coffee table. As we entered the main room with thirty-foot vaulted ceilings, we passed a large glass-enclosed cabinet filled with an assortment of stuffed birds and small dead animals. Lou looked around, but it was evident nobody was there. Lou told me to wait in the car while he tried to find John.

Forty-five minutes later, Lou returned. He came out of a pool house (which I later discovered was John's new recording studio) some fifty yards from the main house. He was alone. He got in the car and didn't say a word.

'How we doin'?' I asked.

'Good.'

I wanted to say, 'How good is good?' but Lou wasn't up for that kind of comedy. If everything went perfectly from here, we were going to be over an hour late. A bit new at this sort of protocol, I was certain that Tanen would never take my call again. The only question left was whether he would even take the meeting once we got to the studio.

Twenty minutes later (and it might have been even longer), John emerged from the main house dressed in a long, colorful Indian robe and wearing his Russian fur hat. Next to him was Michelle Phillips, wearing a similar Indian robe and sandals. She looked pissed off. Michelle was a surprise addition to this meeting, but by this time there was no reason to rock the boat. John motioned that we should go in one of his cars, an old four-door Rolls that was finished in gray primer. John and Lou got in the front seat, and Michelle and I sat in the back. We were just about to drive off when Michelle got out. She told John to wait. She said that she had forgotten something and would be right back. I looked at my watch. It was too late to call.

'What could she have forgotten?' I asked.

'Darvon,' John said.

'Darvon?'

'She has a toothache.'

'Oh . . .'

'We've been burning the candle as they say.'

'Does she know where we're going?'

'Yeah, she wanted to go to the meeting too,' John added.

'Of course she did.'

Ten minutes later, Michelle surfaced. Dropping a Darvon temporarily softened her spirits. She fell asleep in the car before we got to Sunset and stayed asleep until we got to Universal. When we arrived, we were almost two hours late. I wondered whether the guard was even going to let us pass through the gates. Lou, who had not said a word since we left, anticipated my exasperation, turned, looked at the unconscious Michelle, and said, 'Tanen won't mind.'

And Lou was right. As we got off the elevator on the top floor of Universal's black tower, we were not only greeted by Tanen as if we were fifteen minutes early, but he was almost apologetic for the inconvenience. He quickly eyed Michelle, who appeared starkly beautiful while ragged from pain. She walked past him without speaking. He looked at me as if to say I should have been more clever. I should have scheduled this meeting later in the day. Didn't I know that acid, blow, and liquor wasn't conducive to making anyone a 'morning person'? Tanen then thanked John for making the big sacrifice of driving over the hill before lunchtime. John smiled back, forgiving Tanen for putting all of us through such an ordeal. As the entourage proceeded down the hall, every employee on the floor was prepped for their arrival. They all stood up to get a glimpse of the famous rock stars. You could almost hear them humming 'California Dreamin'' when the procession passed their desks.

Tanen's office was backdropped by white walls, had thick, white carpeting with staid European antique furniture. Michelle entered Tanen's office first and immediately threw herself facedown on the couch. John and Lou took their seats without ever referring to Michelle. They continued to wear their hats. Ned took his seat at his desk, the entire San Fernando Valley visible through the floor-to-ceiling window behind him. He leaned back and smiled at the colorful spectacle in front of him. This parade was an executive perk. I looked over at Michelle. Her robe had inched up her legs as she'd tried to get comfortable. She was seductive in her misery.

'Toothache,' I announced to the room, but no one was listening.

What resulted from all of this was not particularly significant. As we fumbled through some brief explanations about a couple of movie ideas, occasionally interrupted by a muffled moan from Michelle as she tried to get more comfortable on the couch, I realized it didn't matter much what was being said. Tanen was intrigued by the players. He was smitten by Michelle. If it wasn't going to cost too much, he was definitely going to explore it. In the end, we walked away with some inexpensive development deal that never resulted in the making of an actual movie. Nonetheless, this story illustrates two things: one, rock stardom packed tons of power in the back rooms at the end of the sixties, and two, more instructively, when you took a meeting in Hollywood, the decision to buy or pass was usually made before the meeting ever took place.

I'd like to say that at this moment I had an epiphany, that I looked around the room and said, 'What a wacky time, I gotta make a movie about this,' but that's not what happened. A few months after this meeting, however, I did run into an old high school mate whom I had not seen in ten years. He couldn't sing, write a song, or play bass, but he had paid the price. From clean-cut, innocuous Jewish kid, he had dramatically mutated into a dashiki-wearing, world-renowned rock publicist strung out on black women and party favors. And, yes, he was wearing a coke spoon around his neck. Over the next few years, I couldn't help but notice that everyone, including me, was irrevocably altered by the times. Irrevocably altered by the music. I was starting to connect the dots. Someday this would be fertile territory for a movie. I put it on hold because I was still trying to figure out how to mix the business of Hollywood with pleasure and still pay the rent. It took twenty-five years for me to pull the trigger. We were in the middle of shooting *Fight Club* when I decided to try to get a script written about some of the people who were hanging out in front of the Whisky A Go-Go way back then—not a movie about the rock stars but a movie about the people who were on the fringe trying to get in.

'If you want to develop this, it's okay with me,' Laura Ziskin said rather matter-of-factly.

'Thanks.'

Laura wasn't quite so perky these days. The trill in her voice had evened out. She was entering her third rocky year as a studio executive, heading up the Fox 2000 division, a pet project of Bill Mechanic's. Before taking this job, Ziskin had had a successful run as a movie producer, but she soon realized that the participation she enjoyed as a 'hands-on' producer would have to be shelved for now. For the most part, directors, writers, and producers simply didn't want her help. Ziskin was left with a mess of bureaucratic details while Mechanic, her boss, was under massive fire from Chernin and Murdoch. Add to that a series of Fox 2000 bombs that were beginning to rain down in buckets (*Inventing the Abbotts, Ravenous, Brokedown Palace*), and Laura was savvy enough to know she might soon be back on the street with the rest of us.

Might as well go with the flow.

'Bill said if we keep the costs down, we should do this,' she said flatly.

'Laura, we can do this, all in, for ten million dollars.'

'Why not?'

'Why not, indeed.'

I didn't know at the time that Cameron Crowe was planning to write and direct a similar movie covering the same period that was going to cost fifty million dollars. No one would be able to write about this period in Hollywood with more power than Cameron. He was there. Both movies were intended to be ensemble pictures. I didn't know it then, but ours was never going to get the same paint job.

There's a producer, a successful producer, who says that he never hires a writer or a director until he watches him walk. If he walks lucky, he hires him. After years of picking wrong, when everything seemed so right, it's only natural that one would resort to a little mojo to get a hit. I'd like to blame the horrible demise of *Sunset Strip* on the first-time director or the well-intentioned writer, but I chose them and I worked with them. I forgot to watch them walk.

Since I can only assume that none of you ever saw this movie, there is no reason to explain it in great detail other than to encourage those of you who are obsessive about movies to try to find this thing in a video bin so you can dissect the making of a bomb. To your surprise, you will see several young, gifted actors (Rory Cochrane, Jared Leto, Anna Friel, Adam Goldberg, and Simon Baker) doing some excellent work. You will hear and see some guitar playing that is impressive. You will see some witty and authentic moments from the seventies that rival anything that has been done of that period. Nonetheless, it fell through the cracks. It didn't walk lucky. Apparently, it didn't have that thing.

We screened it for the taciturn Bob Harper to see what sort of read we would get from marketing.

'What do you think, Bob?'

'I just don't know who it's for.'

'Uh-oh.'

'I don't see the target.'

'Well, why not sell it to those that like it?'

'That's the problem.'

'How so?'

'I'm afraid those that will like it skew older, and the materials, vis-à-vis the cast, is gonna skew younger.'

'How do we know this?'

'The test scores.'

'But the test scores aren't always—'

'And my *gut*.'

'Of course, the gut thing.'

I was fucked. You simply can't argue your way around marketing 'speak.' Fox held the release of *Sunset Strip* for several months. By the time they were ready to come out with it, I was no longer under contract at the studio. Laura Ziskin was back on the street working as a producer for Sony Pictures. Bill Mechanic was unceremoniously dumped by Chernin and Murdoch and was already hanging out in Beverly Hills considering his options. The controversy over *Fight Club* was rumored to be the bullet that finally got him, but the facts don't bear it out. A true malaise had hovered over all of us during the last twelve months. Those providing Bill with movies that were nose-diving into oblivion were not part of an exclusive club. The Fox movie division couldn't buy a hit. It didn't matter what the genre was. Action movies like *Thin Red Line* or *The Siege* disappointed. Smarter fare such as *The Newton Boys* or *Pushing Tin* or *Bulworth* gagged. Big-name stuff like Jodie Foster in *Anna and the King* or Leonardo DiCaprio in *The Beach* or the costly animated *Titan A.E.* were total wipeouts. As the carnage piled up, I would look for telltale signs when I ran into Bill. Little things, such as would there be a slight lisp or stutter in his speech? Or would he be bleeding from his ears while we were eating lunch in the commissary? I gotta say, he handled the avalanche with fatalistic poise, integrity intact.

I was reminded of an old studio head who said to me, shortly after being fired from Paramount, that if he had green-lighted the movies that he had passed on and canceled all of the movies he had agreed to make, he would have ended up in the same place. When his reign ended, he left the place with the humility of knowing that he didn't seem to know anything.

Mechanic told me months later, after denying me the extra money I needed to secure a vibrant seventies sound track, that Fox had decided to cut their losses and put the movie out in only one theater and then they were going to pull it. No matter how you feel about your movie, no matter how small the movie, this sort of news is like getting gutted. There's no response. It's the terminal-cancer call from the doctor, the intimate dread of being caught on the street with nothing on. All you can do is go home and commiserate with your loved ones.

Why bother with one theater? Why not just take the film and make hundreds of guitar picks? Because it was the only credible business decision. Let me explain how this works. In their corporate output deals—with video companies, pay per view, syndications, and cable—the studio gets paid when a movie gets theatrically released. A theatrical release in that deal was triggered when the movie appeared in only one theater (these terms have changed somewhat since, but that was the deal that studios could make then). If they did not put it in one theater, they would not get paid at all. In the case of a small movie that the studio no longer believes in, it's smart business to bite the bullet, get several million dollars back on these output deals, and not risk any further money by investing in a large marketing campaign. Today, the marketing costs to open a movie nationally can soar upward of twenty to thirty million dollars. You've gotta believe.

Ironically, Cameron Crowe's *Almost Famous*, a wonderful movie about the seventies, probably lost more money for DreamWorks than *Sunset Strip* did for Fox. With all the dazzling talent of Cameron, the movie's costs, including marketing, did not bring in sufficient numbers to break out anywhere near even. Between the two of us, making future genre movies about the seventies will inevitably be put on hold.

One of the minor producing lessons from all this is to know that the more money a movie costs, the greater the chance that the studio will be compelled to provide it with a major marketing campaign. It's the only way they can get their big investment back. Expensive movies, even if they don't 'test' well, will always get a big national splash. By this time, the chance that *Sunset Strip* would ever get a legitimate release was zero. It was too cheap, too under the radar, to become a noticeable failure. The remaining executives had no personal investment in the movie. Hell, most of them weren't even aware the movie got made. Fox had nothing to gain other than its erasure.

It disappeared like the morning mist.

FOURTEEN

I'M AS INDEPENDENT AS
A DRY CLEANER FROM LEBANON

'David, you know Tia Carrere?' Elie Samaha asked.

'Uhhh . . .'

David Mamet looked at me over his glasses. Mamet didn't have a clue who she was, but he was being cautious because this might be some sort of quiz he had to pass to get the money for his next movie. We were in an empty Italian dive on Santa Monica Boulevard and La Cienega sitting at a small table next to a reeking open men's room. It was a business lunch. It didn't resemble lunch at Sherry Lansing's table at the Paramount commissary or the special booth next to Barry Diller at the Grill in Beverly Hills, but the intentions were all the same. I found out later, Samaha owned the restaurant.

'You don't know Tia Carrere!'

'How 'bout you?'

'Uh, Latin dancer, right?' I guessed.

'No. Actress.'

'Of course she is.'

'*My Teacher's Wife? Instant Karma?*'

'I think I remember.'

'Do you know why I tell you?'

'No.'

'She's also my recent ex-wife.'

'I'm sorry,' David commiserated.

'Eh, it's okay,' Elie said. He made a fist with his left hand and straightened his forearm simulating a hard-on. He broadened his smile. 'Cost me thirty-two million dollars, but what a, what a —'

'Does that mean you want us to cast her?' I asked.

David sighed.

Let me back up. After leaving Fox, I decided to take the indie route to raise money for *Heist*, a movie Mamet wanted to direct and I wanted to produce. It's not that we didn't want a major studio to fund it, but because of a variety of factors, mainly a series of regrettable turndowns, we were on the street looking for money. We had to put a 'package' together and peddle our wares.

I'm certain that you're about to say, 'Well, I sure hope he didn't try Robert De Niro again and have another one of those god-awful readings.' Of course I did. And for those observant students of Hollywood, you know that history always repeats itself. Do I have to add that after this reading Bob nodded, gave me his famous wrinkled grin, then talked briefly about how good the screenplay was and what a great writer Mamet was? Of course he did. Bob was always respectful. But when we walked outside and he started to tell me what a great producer I was, I knew we were dead. When he shook his head and said, 'I've got a little problem with "the gold," all that talk about "the gold, the gold, the gold." Uh . . . I don't get it.' I was on the raw edge of saying, 'Fuck me, the movie's *about* the fucking gold! Are we all on acid?' But even I was starting to figure this game out. In the vernacular of Hollywood, Bob meant unequivocally no, he'd rather piss in a fountain.

Fortunately, within a few weeks of that rejection, Fred Specktor, the venerable agent from CAA, called Mamet and me and said both Gene Hackman and Danny DeVito had read the script, wanted to work together, and wanted to do the movie. Great news. I'd been trying to corral Hackman for years and had finally got him. Our spirits were temporarily lifted, but some significant hurdles were ahead. The addition of these key elements was a terrific start, but this movie was going to cost substantially more than any movie Mamet had previously directed. As much acclaim as some of his movies had received, the box office results were not significant. We had to convince someone that if Mamet was given a larger budget with a more recognizable cast, he would deliver a movie that would intrigue a larger audience. Being artsy and classy to the studios was euphemistically suicide to the upside. As producer Joel Silver once proudly said, 'I don't make art. If I want art, I'll buy it.' This made him a very endearing fellow in the executive hallways.

The world of independent financing is considerably different from traditional studio financing—different in style as well as in substance. As odd as it sounds, the studio system and the agency system have become gentrified over the last thirty years—more conservative, more polite, and even more ineffective. This was not how it began. Sam Goldwyn was a glove salesman and Harry Cohn started by selling 'hot' furs. Neither of them finished high school. When Lewis Selznick met an old chum, a herring salesman turned movie producer, Lewis told his family, 'Today I met an old friend. He is the dumbest man I ever knew. If he can make money in pictures, anyone can.' Years ago, when Lew Wasserman instituted a tacit dress code of black suits and black ties for the MCA executives to spruce up the dignity a bit, hoping to make his group look like smart-thinking corporate types, he still insisted that all his agents follow the mantra 'Don't smell it. Sell it.' But the times had softened the town. Everyone had been making too much money. It was time to clean up the act. Instead of imitating the outrageous behavior and spirit of the pioneers who had started the business, the players slowly but inexorably started to separate themselves from the past. Like the Jews and African-Americans trying to assimilate to their new country, those with power in Hollywood have quietly been straightening their hair and scooping their noses, trying carefully to fit in to look like those East Coast bankers and intellectuals who never took much notice of them in the first place.

Samaha, dressed in a neatly pressed dark olive suit and tight black T-shirt, recalling the *Miami Vice* pimp fashion of the eighties, removed his jacket. He waved at the cook scurrying around the open kitchen. We were waiting for our food to come. It was 1:30 P.M. but no other tables were occupied.

'David, you have to shoot the movie in forty-five days.'

'I can't.'

'Sure you can.'

'I'll need at least fifty-five days.'

'You must shoot it in Canada. We save lotta money.'

'I'll consider that.'

'Forty-five days.'

'Fifty-five days.'

'How many days you shoot *State and Main*?'

'Thirty.'

'Y'see. I love that movie.'

I tried to momentarily divert the conversation. 'What's with this fucking bathroom, Elie?'

'It's a famous spot.'

'Maybe we should admire it from a different table.'

'This is best table in the place.'

'Aren't you concerned that the heavy Lysol might leak into our salads?'

'I'm not worried.'

'Well, I think it's an issue.'

'Djya know that Jim Morrison OD'd in there years ago?'

'No.'

'Everyone wants this table.'

'Elie, no one's here.'

'Listen, we can move over there by the wall, but this's still the best table in the house.'

Samaha did not go to USC film school. He did not get an MBA from Boston University. He didn't weep at Bertolucci movies. He didn't give a fuck about the Coen brothers. He got here on a different bus. Born in Beirut, he left Lebanon as a teenager and wound up in Manhattan as a bouncer for Studio 54 before migrating to Los Angeles in 1982. Once he hit Hollywood, instead of trying to cozy up to rising directors at the monthly film festivals, he decided the dry cleaning business would be a more direct route to fame and fortune. He opened Celebrity Cleaners, mounted many autographed pictures of celebrities on the wall, and courted the studios' dry cleaning business. He told us at lunch that he found the studios would pay any amount to get their wardrobes cleaned, especially if the service was top-notch. He decided to always stay open on Sundays and always stay open until midnight. Once he got ensconced in the movie business, if he thought an agent or an executive had done him a good turn, he would provide that person with a laminated card that entitled the cardholder to one year of free Celebrity dry cleaning. Make fun of him if you wish, but while the rest of Hollywood was hoping to sit next to Arthur Schlesinger Jr. or Henry Kissinger at some charity ball for the aged, Samaha was on the street hustling models and small-time celebs while he figured out a way to get the money to finance movies.

Through his Franchise Film company, Elie had boldly found a niche. He had figured out a way to finance movies that the major studios were shying away from, yet still make money. What he had come upon was nothing new. Years ago, mavericks like Dino De Laurentiis and Arnon Milchan had discovered a worldwide market that was vast and rich and that with the right kind of schmoozing could be exploited. Some movie stars and a handful of star directors, whether they knew it or not, had an international cachet that meant something. Packaging and selling the talent to the foreign buyers was the combination to the safe. If Samaha could get these key elements to cut their fee for a project dear to their heart as well as convince the producer to cut the cost of filming by scurrying off to a foreign country, Samaha could make a score. With the right package in place, his game was to presell the movie to foreign territories for more than the cost of the movie, leaving no risk, only reward.

Here's an example: Travolta had a pet project, *Battlefield Earth*, that no studio in Hollywood would touch, even though Travolta was enjoying a personal revival at the box office. Perhaps because of its intimate link to L. Ron Hubbard and Scientology, or because science fiction is enormously expensive, or because the project could not attract a bona fide first-class director, Travolta could not get the movie jump-started. Ergo, Samaha smells the opening, calls Travolta up, and declares that the one movie he's dying to make is *Battlefield Earth* starring John Travolta. Travolta at the time was making upward of fifteen million dollars a picture. But this was his labor of love. Samaha knew that if the movie could be made for a certain number, he could sell off most of his financial exposure to international markets before one set was built, one costume sewn. If the movie died, the only ones holding the bag would be the foreign investors, while Elie could dine out on the Travolta connection. Travolta wanted to see this movie made so badly that, apparently, he not only reduced his fee substantially and agreed to limit the cost of production, but also ultimately put up some of his own money to see the damn thing through.

For Elie, this was a perfect fit. Although the movie met a truly grim fate at the box office and an even sadder fate with critics, Travolta made the movie he wanted to make and Elie walked away with money in his pocket. I suppose his foreign partners, once they were able to get up off their knees and wipe the vomit from their shoes, could only hope to get their money back by betting with Samaha on the next one.

From a filmmaker's point of view this is not such a bad situation. Elie doesn't give you script notes, doesn't hand out his opinions on the final cut, and doesn't tamper much with the casting choices of the additional roles. Shit, he might not even have read the script. He leaves the 'making' of the movie to those who can. After years of wading through the silly litany of comments from studio executives whose only film credentials are a leased BMW and a studio job, there's something irresistible about a guy who simply plays it as a businessman. He's gonna fuck you if he can, but it will be just about the money. How long he can pull this off is hard to say.

'I want to make this movie,' Elie said.

'We do too,' Mamet answered.

'I love it.'

'We do too.'

'No, I really love it.'

'That's great,' I added.

'I love Hackman.'

'We do too.'

'And I just had dinner at Danny's house. I love him too.'

'We agree on that.'

'You know, uh, forgive me,' Elie said, punctuating his face with fatigue, 'but I'm a little tired.'

Mamet turned to me with that 'Here comes the bad news' glance.

'I think you look good,' I said.

'Thank you.'

'You're welcome.'

'Last night I was at the Sunset Room, my club, until four in the morning.'

'Elie, you're moonlighting.'

'I was drinking with Sly.'

'That's good.'

'Sly was at *my* table, Don Johnson was three tables down. A real good night.'

The conversation stalled for about ten long seconds.

'David, you want to come to my club tonight?'

'No, thank you,' he said politely.

Another awkward pause.

'You know, David, did I tell you that I made more than sixty films over the last three and a half years?'

'I had no idea.'

'It's true.'

'Really . . . ?'

'I swear.'

'That's a lot of volume,' I said.

'I made a lot of money.'

'I bet.'

'Over sixty movies.'

We were desperately trying to locate some common ground.

'So which ones are your favorites?' David asked.

Elie looked at us carefully. He opened his mouth, but nothing came out. He couldn't quite come up with one title that stood out from the pack. It was like watching a magician in a slump fumbling to pull out the right card. I was trying to help, but I didn't know any of the pictures he had sponsored either. He finally mentioned some movie in the planning stage that he was working on with Billy Zane and director Ted Demme. He said he was proud of that one, but they had yet to start filming. He added that if we wanted to meet Billy Zane, he was also going to be at the club tonight.

'Thanks for the lunch, Elie,' I said, dropping my napkin on the table.

'It was very generous.' David smiled.

'Okay, okay. Let's make it fifty days,' Elie said.

'We'll give it a college try,' I said.

As with all other meetings in Hollywood, the decisions were made before the meeting began. Samaha had already sussed out what the foreign market would bear for a Gene Hackman/Danny DeVito combination with David Mamet at the helm. So long as we committed to the right number, this deal was closed. Predictably, Samaha would make a profit before the movie ever wrapped.

As a final footnote, we ended up shooting *Heist* in fifty-five days.

I arrived at Tana's early. The bar was filling up and the booths were already occupied. For the first time in weeks, I was actually looking forward to meeting with Jerry. I know that the first thing he's going to say when he scans this room is 'Fucking hell, the place is packed and there's nobody here.' I ordered a drink and waited.

Warner Bros., the domestic distributor for *Heist*, had just begun screening the movie for the long-lead press (magazine editors and magazine critics), and the early returns were encouraging. For a film noir filled with violence and irony, it was a nice surprise to watch people warming to it. To top it off, Alberto Barbera, the head of the Venice Film Festival, had called two days before to say that he loved the movie and wanted to invite us to the festival. It was to be the first of many invitations. And, of course, there was something unforgettable about having a front-row seat to watch Gene Hackman (Joe Moore) standing over a critically wounded Danny DeVito (Bergman) at the climactic shoot-out. Bergman, shocked that his life force is ebbing away, asks Moore, 'D'ya want to hear my last words?' Without hesitation Moore blows him away and says, 'I just did.' Mamet served up the meat cold on this one.

Not that everything had gone smoothly during the making of this film. With all of the sacrifices that have to be made when you reach outside the studio system for money, one of the most ludicrous is the impact all of this has on 'producer' credits. In the final credit roll, the audience is mercilessly bombarded with nine producers: three producers, of which I am one with Samaha and one of his partners; three executive producers, all of whom are either Samaha friends and/or employees. Two coproducers. One line producer. And, no, I'm not going to add 'and a partridge in a pear tree.'

Suffice it to say that not only did these people rarely make any producing contributions, but in most cases, neither Mamet or I have ever met them. There's a producers' guild, rising from the ashes, currently trying to sort out this horrible indignity on future films. But it's a troubling thought to assume there's going to be a big outpouring of sympathy for the poor mistreated movie producer. Maybe a league should be created to protect agents who have had their feelings hurt, or maybe some umbrella organization for film executives who sense their time is running out. Ain't it sort of like asking people to cheer for the fox in the henhouse?

I always forget how good the margaritas are at Tana's. I must have gotten distracted because I suddenly realized that Jerry was now forty-five minutes late. I wasn't surprised. He was a no-show. That rat bastard had the antennae of a Siamese cat. He could smell my good news coming from across Coldwater Canyon, and he wanted no part of it. He knew it was time to find a new den and some fresh blood, time to take his black voodoo down the road and piss on some rookie. I should've just walked away, but I decided to give him another few minutes. If he didn't show up, I would call him, leave a blistering message on his answering machine, then get on with it.

I moved to the rear door where I could get better reception from my cell phone.

Trying to compose a message to Jerry, behind three margaritas, wasn't all that easy. All kinds of weird detritus ran through my head. First, I wanted to sour his mood by thanking him for the amateur therapy sessions. I had to let him know that being one of 'les grandes facilitators'—as he sarcastically referred to movie producers—didn't necessarily mean that your arm is laced up to your elbow in Crisco. I wanted to remind him—and this would surely test his stomach— that there's even a parcel of dignity in getting this shit done. Yeah. And by the way, before we get too mawkish, let's not forget the ultimate mantra: It's a helluva way to keep your pool heated.

Arrivederci, baby. Thanks for the memories.

A NOTE ON THE AUTHOR

Art Linson was born in Chicago and grew up in Los Angeles. He has been producing movies for over twenty years, and his credits include *The Untouchables, Heat, Fast Times at Ridgemont High, Scrooged, Fight Club,* and *Heist*. In 1995, he published his first book, *A Pound of Flesh: Perilous Tales of How to Produce Movies in Hollywood*.

A NOTE ON THE TYPE

The text of this book is set in Granjon. This old style face is named after the Frenchman Robert Granjon, a sixteenth-century letter cutter whose italic types have often been used with the romans of Claude Garamond. The origins of this face, like those of Garamond, lie in the late fifteenth-century types used by Aldus Manutius in Italy.